SHAKESPEARE'S
EARLY COMEDIES

SHAKESPEARE'S EARLY COMEDIES

By

E. M. W. TILLYARD

O.B.E., LITT.D., F.B.A.

HUMANITIES PRESS: NEW JERSEY
ATHLONE PRESS: LONDON

Reprinted in 1983 in the United States of America
by Humanities Press Inc., Atlantic Highlands, NJ
and in Great Britain by The Athlone Press by
arrangement with Chatto & Windus Ltd.

Humanities   0 391 02865 0   Paper
             0 391 02864 2   Cloth

Athlone   0 485 30015 X   Paper
             0 485 30014 1   Cloth

MANUFACTURED IN THE UNITED STATES OF AMERICA

CONTENTS

CONTENTS

EDITOR'S PREFACE

A T the time of his death in 1962 my father had written most of a projected work on Shakespeare's early comedies. In addition to the chapters presented here, a chapter on *A Midsummer Night's Dream* and a concluding chapter had been envisaged. There are very few notes for these missing sections, and no indications of the line he would have followed. But the text of the completed parts had been largely revised in readiness for publication, and seemed worth printing. The reader may therefore prefer to consider the book as a set of essays, rather than as a unified whole.

Nevertheless, there might well have been rearrangement and addition within what had been written, and where the author left a memorandum to do something of the sort this has been incorporated as a footnote. In particular the chapter on *The Taming of the Shrew* would probably have received some further treatment, perhaps bringing in some of the material of the Appendix (page 209 ff.), an essay written after the completion of the chapter. It is included here by kind permission of the editor of the Brown University bicentenary volume *Shakespeare 1564–1964: a collection of modern essays by various hands* (Providence, R. I., 1964), for which it was originally commissioned. I am most grateful for the opportunity to add this postscript to the main work.

The text of the plays is that of the Tudor edition of Shakespeare's works, edited by Professor Peter Alexander (Collins, London, 1951), and all act, scene and line references are made to it. In a few places the author evidently preferred a different reading. An asterisk after the line reference indicates that for this reason the quotation deviates in some particular from the Tudor text.

Preparing this work for publication was more complicated than the apparently straightforward result may suggest, and I wish to acknowledge the valuable assistance given at various stages by my mother, my wife, Mrs B. C. F. Wade, and Miss M. S. Couper.

STEPHEN TILLYARD

FOREWORD

OF all that has been written recently on Shake-spearean comedy much is cross-sectional; much has pursued themes, patterns, images, and so on, recurring throughout the sequence of plays. Less has been written about the plays themselves. There are of course the introductions to new editions; and there have been articles on this or that play: but any books surveying the whole sequence of the comedies have done so with some one special matter in mind. Thus, there may be room for a book like this; one that deals with the comedies primarily as plays, as separate entities. But such treatment need not exclude comment on the background and on how one play is linked with another; and I shall not avoid these matters. Further, I shall try to be cross-sectional in a way that may be unusual in the criticism of Shake-speare. This way has to do with a certain theory of the literary kinds. Briefly, I hold that today the only valid theory of the kinds is psychological: that the kinds correspond to parts of the human mind. But though valid, the theory suffers from the drawback that the traditional kinds include varied, even heterogeneous things, and that works habitually given the name of this or that kind turn out, on inspection, to be unexpectedly mixed. This is, of course, especially true of Elizabethan drama, which draws on the medieval inheritance of the romance as well as on the orthodox mode of western European comedy. Thus, expecting multiplicity, I shall, as one preliminary, take the general range of Elizabethan comedy and ask to what parts of the mind it corresponds. Moving on to Shake-speare, I shall seek to relate these correspondencies to this or that play. Though a single ingredient can recur in different plays, he never repeats himself; the mixture is always different. If in dealing with the separate plays I can refer to those parts of the mind over which the romantic drama ranges, I hope to contrive some sort of initial entry into their different natures and at the same time to connect each to each through this common standard of reference. But before I deal with these matters, which will lead directly to the plays themselves, I must write briefly on the background of Shakespeare's comedies.

Chapter I

THE BACKGROUND

i. INTRODUCTION

IN writing on Shakespeare's History Plays I spent over a third of my space on the background. That was sixteen years ago; and, if I were writing a book on the same topic now, the proportions would be different; for in these years that background has become far better known. But in 1945 few had connected the Histories with the current set of ideas on order or on the nature of history or on the stretch of history from Richard II to the Tudors. And to establish these connections convincingly needed plenty of room. There has been no such ignorance about the background of the Comedies, which has been generally familiar for a great number of years.

Not only has the background of the Comedies been covered better than that of the Histories; but it demands different treatment. While conceptions of history greatly affected the way Shakespeare wrote, current critical theory on comedy (of the kind inherited from Donatus) had singularly little bearing on his Comedies. No doubt he sometimes wrote in accord with it; but never through fear, and he blandly ignored it whenever he fancied. Passing from the 'thought' to the literary background, we used to find readers reluctant to admit the wealth of writing to which Shakespeare had access to enrich his Histories. For instance, they pretty well ignored Hall or Fabyan or Froissart in exclusive favour of Holinshed. On the other hand, Shakespeare's multifarious debts to earlier writing, narrative and dramatic, when he wrote his Comedies, have long been recognized. Thus, in writing on the literary background of the Histories I had to plead at length for greater inclusiveness. In contrast, coming to the Comedies, I find that the question is not of *which?* but of *how much of each?*, the question of *which?* having been settled already. To decide how much requires, in the main, tact and intelligent guess-work and certainly not any great length of statement.

Such being the position, I shall confine my discussion of the background of the Comedies to a single chapter.

Trying to formulate Shakespeare's general dealing with his literary background, I can only conclude (what is already self-evident on grounds of psychological probability) that he got his stuff from all over the place, that he was immensely assimilative, and that what he had assimilated he retained for use in a most astonishing manner. In the aggregate most of the source-attributions are correct; where the mistakes occur is in making too much of any one element.

The best way to bring home to oneself that range of literature, whether heard or read, that served Shakespeare in writing his Comedies is to consider what was open to him in the course of his life, taking into account the kind of life he led and the degree of learning that seems to have been his and assuming that he assimilated a big proportion of it. Though by such a method one may go wrong over a detail or two, one will compensate by getting the best picture of the general truth. The more usual way is to begin through his predecessors in the drama, and this has led men to give too little weight to non-dramatic writing. Thus there has till recently been a reluctance to allow Spenser's poems their due or to believe that Shakespeare could have found pleasure in *A Mirror for Magistrates*. Proofs have recently accumulated that he knew these works well; but anyone taking the line I have recommended must have concluded that the probabilities against his not having read them were very great. How could a man of Shakespeare's temper and interests have avoided reading works so overwhelmingly popular? Not that simple guessing from a general knowledge of Tudor literature is enough. We need to be reminded by the experts that much romantic drama, inheriting a tradition as old as the middle of the fifteenth century and written near the time of Shakespeare's birth, has been lost; we need to be told to what Shakespeare was open in his grammar school days; and we need to recall that Shakespeare knew the Bible well and that among other things the Bible is a store of narrative.

The best I can now do is to survey rapidly some of the principal writings or traditions or habits that compose the background of Shakespeare's Comedies.

ii. THE CRITICAL BACKGROUND

The recent fashion for finding all critical wisdom in the curt and cryptic sayings of Aristotle's *Poetics* has its counterpart in that of stressing the scanty pronouncements on comedy made by ancient grammarians and their Italian successors. These in general go back to Donatus, a grammarian of the fourth century A.D. and teacher of St Jerome. Donatus, as well as his Latin grammar, popular throughout the Middle Ages, produced editions of five of Terence's plays and included in them a short account of the beginnings, progress, and nature of Greek and Latin comedy.[1] Looking on Terence's plays as the embodiment of the true comic norm, he lays down such rules as these: that comedy deals with middling people, with small adventures and unturbulent passions; that it avoids history and presents fictitious characters; that it begins with mild dangers and misfortunes and ends in prosperity; that it is strict in assigning a stock garb to a stock character. The Italian critics of the Renaissance mainly repeat Donatus but are at greater pains to assert the moral effect of comedy. Thomas Heywood was perfectly in their tradition when in *An Apology for Actors*[2] he both quotes Donatus on comedy and argues in this fashion on its promoting morality;

> And what then is the subject of this harmless mirth? either in the shape of a clown to show others their slovenly and unhandsome behaviour, that they may reform that simplicity in themselves which others make their sport, lest they happen to become the like subject of general scorn to an auditory. . . . Sometimes they discourse of pantaloons, usurers that have unthrifty sons, which both the fathers and sons may behold to their instructions: sometimes of courtesans, to divulge their subtleties and snares in which young men may be entangled, showing them the means to avoid them.

I cannot see that Donatus and his successors are any great help to our understanding of Shakespeare's Comedies. We were already aware without them that he was familiar with Latin comedy; and to that awareness a knowledge of Donatus adds nothing. The most suggestive things in Donatus are peripheral: namely that Greek comedy goes back to the *Odyssey* and that there were

[1] See P. Wessner's Teubner edition of *Donatus on Terence* (Leipzig, 1902), pp. 15-29.
[2] Edition: London, 1841, p. 54.

14

strict conventions about costume. The range of Shakespearean comedy may be compared with that of the
Odyssey, and later I shall suggest that conventions of dress
may help with our interpretation of a character in the
Merchant of Venice. Heywood's passage likewise is typical
in showing how little related were conventional theory
and dramatic practice in Elizabethan drama. It is nicely
calculated to head us off so typical a comedy as Heywood's
own *Maid of the West*.

I do not mean to say that we should not distinguish
between the 'rival traditions' as propounded by Harbage[1]
or deny the existence of the two kinds of comedy between
which Miss Bradbrook[2] tells us Shakespeare had ultimately to choose or the contrast that Coghill[3] stresses
between the Donatan-Jonsonian and the medieval-
Shakespearean types. What I mean is that such distinctions have little to do with current critical theory. The
example of Terence may have meant much but the supporting theory of Donatus meant little. Thus there were
imperative dramatic habits, but a close kinship such as
that between the practice of Racine and the critical tone of
Rapin simply does not exist in the Elizabethan tradition.
Even with the typical work of the most academic of all
the great English comedy-writers, Jonson, the Donatan
kind of criticism is no great help; it is hopelessly irrele-
vant to the Marlovian monstrosities that give it its nature
and its merits.

Again, I do not wish to imply that recent work on the

[1] A. B. Harbage, *Shakespeare and the Rival Traditions* (New York,
1952).
[2] M. C. Bradbrook, *The Growth and Structure of Elizabethan Comedy*
(London, 1955), p. 78.
[3] N. Coghill, *The Basis of Shakespearean Comedy*, the first essay in *Essays
and Studies* of the English Association, 1950.

critical background of Elizabethan drama has been wasted. For long our knowledge of it was scrappy; and Madeleine Doran's *Endeavors of art*,[1] to name only one example of recent work on the topic, has effected a long overdue clarification.

iii. THE NARRATIVE BACKGROUND

Most recent critics of the Comedies have proclaimed the importance of the sheer story with its attraction for simple folk. W. W. Lawrence goes so far as to say that

> the course of most of Shakespeare's plays was governed in the beginning by the adoption of an old tale and of the conventions bound up with it—a very different procedure from that of the dramatist who builds his play about a character, and makes plot illustrative of character and subordinate to it.[2]

And one of the ways of entering the world of Shakespeare's Comedies is to remember the wealth of narrative matter open to all classes of the community. Although the better educated knew more kinds of story, a big area was common to all classes. The fourteenth chapter of the second book of Sidney's *Arcadia* provides an emblem of this state of affairs. There we find the homely Miso and her daughter Mopsa sharing the story-telling exercises of their betters, Pamela, Philoclea and Zelmane. After hearing the romantic story of Erona, Miso is allowed to tell her old wives' tale, which she prefaces with

> I will tell you now, what a good old woman told me, what an old wise man told her, what a great learned clerk told him and gave it him in writing; and here I have it in my prayer-book.

---

[1] *Endeavors of art: a study of form in Elizabethan drama* (Madison, 1954).
[2] *Shakespeare's Problem Comedies* (New York, 1931), p. 14.

Then they 'draw cuts' to decide who shall tell the next
story; and 'blind Fortune gave Mopsa the pre-eminence'.
She begins thus:

> In time past there was a king, the mightiest man in all his
> country, that had by his wife the fairest daughter that did ever eat
> pap. Now this king did keep a great house, that every body
> might come and take their meat freely. So one day, as his daughter
> was sitting in her window, playing upon a harp, as sweet as any
> rose and combing her hair with a comb all of precious stones,
> there came a knight into the court upon a goodly horse, one hair
> of gold and the other of silver; and so the knight, casting up his
> eyes to the window, did fall into such love with her that he grew
> not worth the bread he ate, till many a sorry day going over
> his head, with daily diligence and grisly groans he wan her affec-
> tion, so that they agreed to run away together. And so in May,
> when all true hearts rejoice, they stale out of the castle without
> staying so much as for their breakfast.

That Mopsa's story (cut short by Philoclea) should be a
parody of the still popular romances like *Huon of Bordeaux* or *Palmerin of England* does not queer the evidence
Sidney's passage gives for a common area of story. In the
same way the lines in Milton's *L'Allegro* about the tales
told when darkness has fallen 'of many a feat', of Fairy
Mab and Robin Goodfellow, present another area of
story common to the whole community. A third area, often
forgotten in thinking of Elizabethan drama, is the Old
Testament. Its stories, as well as being sacred, formed a
part of the great repository of narrative which was the
endowment of the humblest of the Elizabethans. And we
should look on a play like Peele's *David and Bathsabe* not
as something exceptional but as issuing naturally out of
that great common repository.

Re-inforcing romance, folk-tales, and the Bible were the

B 17

stories of new knowledge of the physical world. A. H.
Thorndike, who has described so well the multiplicity of
all the happenings true or feigned of which the Elizabethans were aware, writes:

> The progress of knowledge was picturesque adventure. The
> world of today, of actuality, of business, was crossed by reports
> from Florida and Constantinople. The reflections of the most
> stolid apprentice must have been shot by some visions of unknown
> but appealing worlds beyond his ken.[1]

Such being the state of mind of the groundlings, no wonder if the popular comedy sought to satisfy the appetite
for story.

With an equal zest for a story the educated Elizabethans of the time of Shakespeare's earlier comedies com-
manded a wonderfully wide and varied repertory of narrative. Here are some of the strains that reinforced what I
have just described as common property of the community.

First, there is classical narrative, which meant pre-
eminently Ovid, whether absorbed at school and college
in the original, or through a medieval adaptation such as
Gower's, or through Golding's *Metamorphoses*. Here were
marvels indeed but neatly and elegantly presented and fit
for a sophisticated taste. Then, there was the Greek
romance, again feeding the taste for romantic adventure
but less tangled and inconsequent than *Huon* or *Amadis* or
any other typical romance from the library of Don
Quixote. Three of the Greek romances were well known
to the Elizabethans, with the *Aethiopian History* of Helio-
dorus the most valued. Its plot is full of familiar motives:

---

[1] A. H. Thorndike, *English Comedy* (New York, 1929), p. 44.

a pair of lovers, one a princess lost in infancy, are separated, captured by pirates, tested for their chastity, con-
demned to death and so on, till their final reunion. There
are a perfectly upright king and a wicked and lustful
princess among the characters. Sidney owed much to the
Aethopian History in *Arcadia*, as Spenser owed much to
other Greek romances in the sixth book of the *Faerie
Queene*. Sometimes a Greek romance got into medieval
literature through a Latin version and survived after the
original was lost. This is so with the Apollonius story,
which Shakespeare knew through Gower's re-telling and
used in the *Comedy of Errors* at the beginning and in
Pericles near the end of his dramatic career. But this need
not mean that Shakespeare's knowledge of the Greek
romance ended there.

A vast amount of medieval narrative matter got
through, in whatever form, to the Elizabethans. That
form could range from the sophisticated recreations of
Ariosto and Spenser to popular adaptations in chap-
books and ballads. In between were the actual works
that remained current: such as those of Malory and *Palmerin*. Add to these the collections of stories, retold by
Boccaccio and Chaucer or assembled in translation by
Painter. Add also the fables of Geoffrey of Monmouth
concerning the early history of Britain; still popular, witness the latest additions to *A Mirror for Magistrates*. Some
knowledge of the great tradition of medieval allegorical
narrative must have been common, or Spenser could
never have planned the *Faerie Queene* as he did, or Sidney
treated the education of the lover in *Arcadia*. The
Romance of the Rose was available in translation in Thynne's
Chaucer and may or may not have been widely read. We
must certainly not assume that Shakespeare was ignorant

of it.[1] The critics include *Piers Plowman* in their lists of medieval classics.

The Italian *novella*, however much founded on medieval material, demands a paragraph to itself, for it supplied a brevity and a tartness to narrative that was new. We are too apt to confine the importance of such a collection of Italian novels as Painter's *Palace of Pleasure* to its function as a repertory of plots. In this we greatly err, for it is vastly important through its narrative matter in a tight sophisticated form. I will here record my impression that Shakespeare owed more to the Italian novel than to any other precedent (the plays of Lyly included) for his method in fashioning a drama out of narrative material.

iv. THE DRAMATIC BACKGROUND

By being emphatic on what Shakespeare owed to narrative precedent I do not wish to scant what he owed to the dramatic. It would be ridiculous to minimize his debt to Terence; and yet he had to get away from Latin comedy in order truly to find himself. And Ovid may have ended in being the stronger influence. To the medieval drama the debt of Elizabethan drama and hence of Shakespeare in particular was enormous. I refer not only to specific plays, which were of the later kinds of Morality and Interlude but even more to the medieval inheritance of the mixed play, of the freedom to set the serious and the ridiculous side by side. The most direct examples of this inheritance are seen in tragedy, where highly serious matter exists alongside the comic. In comedy it is a case not so much of mixing the serious and the trivial as of

---

[1] See J. Vyvyan, *Shakespeare and the Rose of Love* (London, 1960).

mixing the fantastic and the realistic. But the great thing
was that through the medieval inheritance Shakespeare
was free to concoct the mixture that suited him. That his
nature impelled him to mix is evident from the very
beginning, for in the *Comedy of Errors*, probably his
earliest surviving comedy and certainly the one most
mindful of classical precedent, the typical Shakespearean
mixture is unmistakably there even if in a minor form.
To the details of late medieval drama Shakespeare owed
less than to his inheritance of the great early mode; but
to say this is not to deny that the Morality theme of the
man haled this way and that by the forces of good and
evil and the Vice from the Interlude made their contrib-
ution.

It is difficult to assess the sway of Italian comedy.
Probably it reinforced rather than originated. In its
learned form it reinforced its Latin originals. Thus Gascoigne's *Supposes*, derived from Ariosto, derived in turn
from Latin comedy, did not begin anything new; and it is
probable that when a dramatist was less conventional and
used romantic material he made less impression on the
Elizabethans than the narrative writers when they behaved in the same way.

Coming to English comedy I welcome recent exhorta-
tions to remember that the habit of dramatizing the matter of the medieval romance goes back to the fifteenth
century at least, that it flourished greatly in the middle of
the sixteenth century, and that it survived in its primitive
form till much later. Medieval examples exist through
hearsay only. Two or three, and notably *Clyomon and
Clamydes* and *Common Conditions*, survive, out of what was
probably a large number, from the third quarter of the
sixteenth century; while *Mucedorus*, dating probably from

early in the nineties, is in the tradition.[1] Even Chapman in his early *Blind Beggar of Alexandria* is not far off it in the romantic, non-comic, part of that play. Moreover *Clyomon and Clamydes*, though written much earlier, was printed in 1599, a testimony to the prolonged popularity of this primitive type of play. The matter of such plays, apart from the Vice (Common Conditions is the Vice and gives his name to the play), is pure romance. Juliana, the Danish princess, will marry Sir Clamydes if he kills a flying dragon which feeds on fair ladies. Alexander the Great is an incidental character. Bryan Sans Foy is a cowardly boaster who puts Clamydes to sleep by enchantment and steals his dragon's head. Princess Neronis dresses as a page to escape the attentions of the King of Norway. In *Common Conditions* characters come and go in a forest, by their diversity reminding one of the characters in Shakespeare's Arden but by the inconsequence of their adventures doing the very opposite. A suspicious tyrant, an unexplained Spaniard and his daughter, and pirates are among the characters. The plot is an unrelated series of marvels. The verse varies from fourteeners to doggerel. *Mucedorus*, in the Shakespearean Apocrypha,[2] is more civilized, less tangled and inconsequent, and in blank verse. Also a pleasant aura of good will invests it. But, fundamentally, it is just surprise stuff, like the two earlier plays; and, like theirs, its true function is to take simple people out of themselves and give them a holiday from the routine of life. When we remember that this kind of comedy prevailed in Shakespeare's early and most

[1] See M. C. Bradbrook, op. cit., pp. 16, 24. Madeleine Doran, op. cit., pp. 299–300, gives an account of *Clyomon and Clamydes* and *Common Conditions*. The first play has been reprinted by the Malone Society, ed. Greg (1913), the second by the Elizabethan Club, ed. Tucker Brooke (New Haven, 1915).   [2] Ed. Tucker Brooke (Oxford, 1908).

impressionable years, we should not hesitate to put it high among the things that compose the background of his comedy.

Of Shakespeare's immediate predecessors in comedy the most important are Lyly, Peele, and Greene. No doubt he owed a considerable debt to them; but on its extent men will continue to disagree.

That Shakespeare in his early plays was directly inspired by specific plays of Lyly, as T. W. Baldwin in his *Shakspere's Five-Act Structure*[1] would have it, I am not convinced. I prefer the notion that Lyly's principal example was more general: and that it was one of style. Lyly set a new standard of verbal artistry; he added a new and higher euphony to the old rhetorical obligations. In his best passages Lyly makes us feel that it is not enough just to obey these obligations; they must be forgotten in the beauty of the final product. And this beauty beyond rhetoric was available to Shakespeare as an example. Take this sentence from *Campaspe*, in which Apelles describes his love:

> Now must I paint things unpossible for mine art but agreeable with my affections: deep and hollow sighs, sad and melancholy thoughts, wounds and slaughters of conceits, a life posting to death, a death galloping from life, a wavering constancy, an unsettled resolution. (III, v)

Here every effect is carefully weighed. For instance, Lyly writes '*mine* art' but '*my* affections' because he knows that the monosyllable, *art*, needs to be supported by the more sounding form of the attached pronoun, while *affections* should not thus be supported. And the resulting beauty prevents his dutiful use of amplification and oxymoron from obtruding. As an example to Shakespeare, Lyly's improved

[1] Urbana, 1947.

23

standard of verbal artistry corresponds to the improved standard of structural skill found in the Italian *novella*.

Peele's influence seems to be slighter. His verse is less sophisticated than Lyly's prose. But it can rise to a lyric power; and Shakespeare may well have been impressed by Oenone's complaint in III, 1, and Paris's oration in IV,1, of the *Arraignment of Paris*, both in blank verse. It may be too that Peele's *Old Wives' Tale* helped him to be able to make fun of the romantic comedy of his youth. Greg in the preface to his Malone Society edition of *Clyomon and Clamydes* considered Peele's play to burlesque this mode. It may to some extent, but rather it burlesques every kind of romantic gadget. For instance, at the end there occurs the episode of Jack's ghost and Eumenides. Eumenides has promised Jack that he will always go shares with him after the fashion of true friends and then in his turn orders Jack to fulfil his corresponding obligation by bisecting his Delia. Jack, putting friendship before love, makes as if to obey. Here Peele burlesques a motive that is typical of the Italian Renaissance as much as of the Middle Ages and which does not occur in *Clyomon and Clamydes*.

It is uncommonly difficult to assess Shakespeare's debt to Greene. There are many passages of Greene that remind one of Shakespeare. And yet I get the impression that the two are parallel rather than in succession, that Shakespeare independently does better some of the things that Greene does worse. Consider Greene's most ambitious play, *James IV*. Dorothea, the English princess who marries the Scottish king, constantly reminds us of Imogen and Richard II's queen. Take scene IV, iv, showing Dorothea, disguised as a squire, with her attendant Nano. Nano wants to cheer her up by a song; and their conversation is much like that in the scene in *Richard II* where the queen's ladies vainly suggest various amusements to distract her from her sorrow. Yet I doubt any connection and would seek influences elsewhere. First, here was a modern playwright going to an Italian *novella* (from Cinthio) for his plot; and who knows but he may have encouraged Shakespeare to do the same? And second, the scale of some of Greene's scenes is larger than that of his contemporaries'. For instance, there is almost a grandeur in the development of the opening scene from its prosperous beginning just after the wedding of James and Dorothea to its end with the villain Ateukin authorized to procure the love of the Countess Ida for the already faithless Scottish king. It is just possible that this largeness of scale helped Shakespeare when in the *Two Gentlemen of Verona* and *Romeo and Juliet* he was in the act of proving himself master of the massive scene. Greene's other plays are less apt than *James IV*. *Friar Bacon and Friar Bungay* has been over-praised. In particular the plotting is not as good as has been maintained, the connection between the two plots being tenuous. The play's virtue is its speed, Greene pushing merrily on with his inorganic stuff. *Orlando Furioso*, nominally founded on Ariosto but actually reverting to the most naïve kind of romantic material, is interesting in joining with *Mucedorus* in prolonging the comic mode of Shakespeare's youth. *The Pinner of Wakefield* with its heart in the right place and its popular royalism may have inspired the *Shoemaker's Holiday* but seems wide of Shakespeare.

V. THE ANTHROPOLOGICAL BACKGROUND

In 1916 Janet Spens published a book called *An Essay on Shakespeare's Relation to Tradition*. It deals principally with

Shakespeare's susceptibility to the folklore on which he had been reared, with his debt to the example of Munday, who in his plays combined the fabulous with the human, and with the influence of folk-plays on the comedies themselves. She was much under the sway of E. K. Chambers's *Mediaeval Stage* at the time of writing. This quotation gives some idea of the tone of her book:

> Shakespeare always took old matter, at first purely literary, such as older plays, English and foreign—and he continued to use such matter to the end. But soon he learned to mix his literary matter with old folk-dramas, which had the vitality of countless generations in them, and their roots in the far-off mysterious kinship between man and the dumb earth with which his dust mingles in death.[1]

Munday was obsessed with the Robin Hood stories, and Miss Spens thinks that from Munday Shakespeare may have got his notion of free woodland life as pictured in the *Two Gentlemen of Verona* and *As you Like It*.[2] Coming to the plays themselves, she finds traces of all the five primitive festivals detected by E. K. Chambers as surviving into the Middle Ages under a superficial Christian garb, even maintaining that after the *Two Gentlemen* Shakespeare habitually took the folk-play for the nucleus of his comedies. Here are some of the details with which she seeks to corroborate her case: the serpent in *As You Like It* derives from the dragon of the folk-plays, while Jaques, always there when the huntsmen sing, represents the leader of the morris-dance; in *Twelfth Night* Sir Toby is the Lord of Misrule; in the *Midsummer Night's Dream* is seen the trace of the ritual mating at night in the fields and of the ass-headed fool who dances with the Lady of May,

[1] pp. 2–3.   [2] pp. 33 ff.

a medieval motive. In the *Merchant of Venice*, Antonio, an addition to the sources, is the primitive scapegoat. It would be unfair to Miss Spens to suggest that she makes the folk-element the only one in Shakespeare's maturer comedies, for she defines their kind as 'the combination of a story having a marvellous element with the delineations of characters intensely human, often erring, sometimes ridiculous, but always drawn with a sympathy that provokes smiles rather than sarcastic laughter, and suggests a fundamental goodwill and harmony in life.'[1] I quote this, as I say, in justice to Miss Spens, not because the generally marvellous is the topic of this section.

Miss Spens has had successors. Northrop Frye has much to say on Comedy in his *Anatomy of Criticism*[2] and something on Shakespeare's Comedies. His treatment is typical of his gifts in its great learning, brilliant presentation, fertile imagination, and bewildering ramification. He writes at greatest length on Comedy's social function but he also connects Comedy with the 'mythos of spring', and it is here that the anthropological passages occur. A single quotation from his remarks on Shakespeare's Comedies will be sufficient illustration for my purposes; it of course does not do justice to Frye's total treatment of the topic of comedy:

> Shakespeare's type of romantic comedy follows a tradition established by Peele and developed by Greene and Lyly, which has affinities with the medieval tradition of the seasonal ritual-play. We may call it the drama of the green world, its plot being assimilated to the ritual theme of the triumph of life and love over the waste land. In the *Two Gentlemen* the hero Valentine becomes captain of a band of outlaws in a forest, and all the other characters are gathered into this forest and become converted. . . .

[1] p. 13.   [2] Princeton, 1957.

The forest in this play is the embryonic form of the fairy world of the *Midsummer Night's Dream*, the Forest of Arden in *As You Like It*, Windsor Forest in the *Merry Wives*, and the pastoral world of the mythical sea-coasted Bohemia in the *Winter's Tale*. . . . In the *Merchant of Venice* the second world takes the form of Portia's mysterious house at Belmont, with its magic caskets and the wonderful cosmological harmonies that proceed from it in the fifth act.[1]

And in the *Merry Wives* Frye detects in Falstaff most of the marks of a vegetation-spirit.

The most thorough-going attempt to interpret Shakespearean comedy through the folk-festival is C. L. Barber's *Shakespeare's Festive Comedy*.[2] He holds that this comedy is Saturnalian, more akin to Aristophanes than to Latin comedy, and that it is best understood in terms of a holiday; the whole experience of one of Shakespeare's comedies is like that of a revel. The various folk-festivals were still alive, the twelve days of Christmas being the longest. The play most directly derived from the festivals was *A Midsummer Night's Dream*. Details derived from the festivals are, for instance, Rosalind's mock-wooing with Orlando, corresponding to a Disguising with its accompanying licence; Sir Toby as Misrule actually following the pattern of contemporary revels at Twelfth Night; and the bicker of Beatrice and Benedick being modelled on Easter Smacks and Hock-tide abuse between the sexes. These are some of the things that Barber says; of course they merely illustrate the subject of this section, they do not, as here presented, give a fair notion of the kind of book Barber has written.

Before commenting on the kind of opinion these three books represent I must make a distinction: that between

[1] pp. 182–3.   [2] Princeton, 1959.

primitive modes of thought and primitive acts of ritual. The first have been the subject of writings by Jung, Gilbert Murray, Maud Bodkin, and have found famous expression in a few words in A. E. Housman's *Name and Nature of Poetry*,[1] where he said of certain lines of Milton that they have so powerful an effect

> because they are poetry, and find their way to something in man which is obscure and latent, something older than the present organization of his nature, like the patches of fen which still linger here and there in the drained lands of Cambridgeshire.

Granted that such modes of thought exist, then, if any Elizabethan poet, Shakespeare was familiar with them. Doubtless Miss Spens, Northrop Frye, and C. L. Barber would agree; but they go much further, doing something very different when they assert that medieval folk-festivals, based on ritual, were a major influence on Shakespeare's Comedies. To have any paramount significance, to be worth serious distinction from the general instinct for periodical jollification, these festivals must remain what they once were: pieces of ritual intended to lead to practical results. I am most doubtful of their so remaining in the age of Chaucer and feel certain they did not by the time of Shakespeare. They served well enough as means of periodical amusement; they were still part of life; but as applied to literature they are too generalized in significance to help our understanding of it. In fact I am impelled to ask the three critics: *nonne entia multiplicastis?* or *are your connections really necessary?*[2]

[1] Cambridge, 1933, p.46.

[2] There is a better initial chance of a genuine connection between folk-drama and Shakespeare's drama in tragedy; between folk-plays of death and revival and those tragedies that imply some sort of rebirth in the mind of the hero and in the society pictured.

Take a few examples. While it cannot be proved that Sir Toby Belch was not suggested by his aptitude to the season which gave its name to the play in which he figures, can we be certain that in a play composed at another time and for ordinary performance at a public theatre a Sir Toby would not have appeared? Is not his type near enough to stock to be likely to occur in any play throughout the calendar? Then again, could Miss Spens produce the least concrete evidence that Antonio is related to the scapegoat? Have we, as we read, the least sense of his benefiting Venice by bearing its sins? For myself, I detect no trace of primitive superstition in Antonio's melancholy and would explain it through contemporary or modern psychology alone. Frye connects comedy with spring, which is furnished with its proper festivals, because it shows something new and fresh in the young generation's asserting itself against the old: but why not connect it with dawn, which is not so furnished with festivals, for the same reasons? And must we really connect Valentine and his robbers in the wood with the green world and the ritual theme of life triumphing over the waste land? Outlaws have always taken to the forests for practical reasons; and why should the little *maquis* of the *Two Gentlemen* differ in kind from the larger one of 1943? Besides, Shakespeare need not have gone to medieval sources for his original; he could have found it in the Greek novel. Barber equates Shylock and Malvolio with the typical misfit of the revels, the butt of the revellers because he will not join in. But surely such a character is a constant in human society and need not be equated with a special manifestation of it. When Margery Kempe travelled with her fellow-pilgrims from Venice to the Levant she showed herself a misfit by weeping when her companions wished to be merry together and exclaiming 'How merry we shall be in Heaven.' But she did not thereby qualify as the original of Shylock and Malvolio.

All this is not to deny that the folk-festivals with their ritual hinterland were a part of Elizabethan life. Indeed they are not quite dead yet. There is something in the ardour of simple women over spring-cleaning beyond mere house-pride, going back to rituals of purification. But then Elizabethan life was immensely varied; and we must beware of giving to a minor element in this variety a weight it does not possess.[1]

[1] There is good commonsense on this same topic as it touches *Sir Gawain and the Green Knight* in Morton W. Bloomfield's article on the poem in *P.M.L.A.* 1961, pp. 14–15. He holds that though in the fourteenth century (as now) pagan ritual survived, its meaning had been forgotten. There is no specific evidence of a *rite de passage* in the poem 'unless all testing is to be regarded as a type of *rite de passage*'.

Chapter II

THE RANGE OF
SHAKESPEARE'S COMEDY

i. THE LITERARY KINDS

I HAVE said that only a psychological theory of the literary kinds will mean much at the present time. Still, there are other theories that have a right to exist, even if they now leave us cold. For instance, there are the distinctions of metre. You cannot hold that the Limerick as a metrical entity does not exist: likewise the more dignified modes of the Sonnet, Rondeau, and Ballade. You are free to go further and declare that a certain metre favours a certain kind of sentiment and banishes others. It would be inappropriate to write a didactic poem on the problem of free will in the metre of the Limerick, while the Sonnet has habitually provoked serious and weighty thoughts.

Another distinction is that of nominal subject-matter. You can distinguish the Heroic Poem as a composition in verse dealing with high action, Pastoral as a composition about the doings and words of shepherds. Here you are safe enough but you do not get far because the range of essential character within these kinds is so vast as to rob the titles of any significance: *Jabberwocky* and *Beowulf* have heroic subjects without being greatly alike. I cannot see this distinction by nominal subject-matter finding favour with the exacting critical spirit of today.

Then there are the vague labels, Drama, Verse Narra-

---

[1] I have given my opinions on the literary kinds at greater length in my *English Epic*, pp. 4–15, and *Epic Strain in the English Novel*, pp. 9–24.

tive, Prose Fiction; useful enough in their unpretentious way but too superficial to satisfy.

But you can think of the literary kinds in two more important ways. You can think of certain areas of literature empirically as centres of compelling, at times tyrannous, convention, where tradition and the rules of the game are supreme. Historically such a way of thinking is of the first importance. It is a fact of literary history that the conventions of the classical epic made poets write in a certain way. For instance, the things that Statius had to say were unlike those that Virgil had to say; and yet it is a fact of literary history that the traditional epic structure that Virgil used and which suited him forced itself unnaturally on Statius. Again, in the age of Elizabeth there were powerful conventions governing the way a tragedy on the topic of revenge should be conducted; and unless you take these into account you will not understand what Shakespeare was doing in *Titus Andronicus*. But the importance of these centres of convention belongs mainly to the past; the only kind to which it applies today being Detective Fiction. For a living theory of the literary kinds we must go elsewhere.

This brings me to the only notion that is likely to commend itself today, namely the psychological one: the notion that there are permanently recurrent propensities or patterns of the human mind and that the literary kinds embody these. There are several reasons why people should distrust the notion. First, it conflicts with the others I have mentioned, and these, though retaining little positive life, are sufficiently established to make what counters them unwelcome. Take, for instance, this conflict. In conventional parlance *King Lear* ranks as a tragedy, *Lycidas* as a pastoral, and the *Ancient Mariner* as a ballad. But recently tragedy has been put in terms of the mental experience of rebirth, which all these three works have been held to embody. This new notion is in itself more congenial to the modern mind than the old but it is unfamiliar still and cannot as yet compete with something less congenial and more familiar. Next, the terms in use are multivocal when it comes to describing the processes of the mind. It may well be that tragedy renders the mental experiences of rebirth, but it certainly renders other experiences also; and we lack the vocabulary to cope with this situation. A theory lacking technical terms and expressible only through arbitrary circumlocutions is at a disadvantage, to say the least. And lastly to define the literary kinds thus psychologically is to run all sorts of risk, is to leave restricted safety for a realm where conjecture, including the most insane, has every chance of flourishing. Nevertheless I believe that the notion of the kinds can still promote the business of criticism and that of the different notions the psychological one stands the best chance of ultimate acceptance.

ii. THE NATURE OF COMEDY

First, let me make clear the meaning of this heading: for it could mean two things equally well; the nature of those mental states that have been pictured in the plays named comedies (for instance, the plays thus named in the First Folio) or the nature of the mental state that has the best right to be called the Comic. Actually I have both meanings in mind. I wish to point to the variety of mental states with which plays called comedies have been concerned and to include among those states the preponderant one. I know of no better account of the state of

34

THE RANGE OF SHAKESPEARE'S COMEDY

mind central to comedy than that given by L. J. Potts in his *Comedy*,[1] He introduces it through the contrasted idea of tragedy:

> I connect the essential distinction between tragedy and comedy with two opposing impulses deeply rooted in human nature. Until we can find a way of reconciling the antinomy in our nature we are all torn between the desire to *find* ourselves and the desire to *lose* ourselves. . . . We are impelled to preserve and accentuate and glory in our separate lives; we believe that every member of our species has his particular and distinct destiny. . . . This natural pride of man and in man I believe to be the psychological foundation of tragedy. . . . But if there is a proper human pride there is a proper human modesty. . . . We cherish our separateness jealously; but we need also to merge it in the life of the world into which we were born, to mix with other people, to adjust our wills and even our characters to the *milieu* in which by choice or necessity we live to the general laws of nature.

And this second impulse is the psychological foundation of comedy. Or one can say that tragedy concerns the individual man's relations to the sum of things, comedy his relations to his neighbour or society. Comedy assumes that society must be made to work, that creatures must somehow learn to live together. It is indeed a deeply rooted doctrine; it even ante-dates man. Len Howard in her *Living with Birds* describes the social laws under which birds have agreed to live. Occasionally they break them; and the chief offender in her own observation was a female blackbird she had named Star. And she comments, 'If every bird acted like Star, there would be pandemonium in their nesting affairs.' So even among birds society must assert itself; and human comedy has to do with this fundamental assertion. Alter the name of Star to Katherina

[1] London, 1949, pp. 16–18.

35

and the bird to a young woman; then cause her to conform to the laws of society; and you find yourself in the centre of the comic norm.

Within the norm there are of course many options of emphasis. A writer can be positive and therefore probably genial. He can show a Portia living up to her principles of mercy and goodwill in society and trying to persuade others to act on them. Or he can present the spectacle of a man or men at odds with society through selfishness or pride or lack of adaptability or what not, and of how they are brought to heel. For instance he can present young men, pretending they can do without women for several years, shown up for what they are worth; or a rigid father expecting a son to have the same tastes as himself and running into trouble and having to revise his expectations. Or a writer can move towards a realm of the mind bearing another name, Satire, and show a bad man offending against society, even preying on it, until at last he is found out and punished.

Such, in brief, is the central area of comedy; and the majority of plays called comedies fall within it. But there are comedies belonging elsewhere; and I must go on to those other places.

Many people have sought to understand and define comedy through the human habit of laughter. I agree with L. J. Potts that this is a wrong procedure. There may be no comedies that do not in one place or another make us laugh, but there are many in which laughter does not at all prevail. For another thing there are many sorts of laughter; and a literary kind that exploited them all would have no central principle. The occasion of my life most violently provocative of laughter (although I did not yield to the provocation) was this. I was once involved in a suicide that imposed on me a sleepless and emotionally harrowing night followed by the duty, early next morning, of identifying the body. As I was leaving the room where the body lay, a man came forward and rewarded me with a shilling. I can see no connection between the ludicrousness of this act and the part of the mind to which comedy appeals. Thus, unless you can say what sort of laughter is in question, you will have no chance of finding the nature of comedy by that approach. Nor will definition ultimately help, for laughter is not the end but only the frequent accompaniment of comedy. The kind of which a certain sort of laughter is the end is called Farce. And that sort is the way we respond to situations violently at odds with the normal run of life. Such laughter is refreshing because it gives us a complete holiday from things as they are. A dream can provoke it as well as a play; and who has not felt the better for an acutely incongruous dream? Farce occurs frequently within true comedies; and the connection is that its incongruous and impossible situations are contrived out of the ordinary traffic of human life; out of such simple human acts as mistaking one man for another or someone else's bedroom for your own. Its setting is society though it is far from being about society; yet as comedy can contain farce, so farce can contain matter about society. Farce admits much fantasy, even the wildest; but if fantasy gets too far from the human scene it fails to provoke laughter and approaches the non-risible area of Romance. I know that I have entered a complex matter, for animals can be the subjects or the victims of situations that men have found farcical. I have not the space to say more about it; but I believe the distinction I have made is roughly true.

Further elements included in plays named comedies

37

but different from the central comic element can be got at through considering the word *Picaresque*. This should indicate a story about a rogue but in actual practice it is multivocal and calls into play more than one motion of the mind. First, there is sympathy with the underdog, the little man, combined with a flattering awareness of our own superiority. He must not be an utter failure but he must be less well placed than the average; he must have his adventures and must just, and only just, survive them. One of the picaresque heroes in this mode was called Brer Rabbit and another Good Soldier Schweik. And Charlie Chaplin re-embodied him in several films. He is important to us because of his wide affinities. He easily lends himself to farcical incident but he is never truly farcical because he retains our sympathy. And on another side he stirs our deeper feelings because there is a little of the scapegoat in him. Through his misadventures may not our own be just a little alleviated? And have not primitive people been prone to approximate the simpleton and the saint?

But, second, the Picaresque can stir another, different, motion of the mind; namely the desire to shed the burdens of duty to self and society without paying too severe a price. Consider the universal fascination of the forgery, whether in art or literature. We love to watch other people doing what we should like to do ourselves but from which fear or scruples head us off; we enjoy the defiance of law or society by proxy. In this sense the Picaresque is anti-comedy; and because it is so, it combines with comedy easily enough. In fact, more often than not anti-comedy gives way to comedy. For, however much we enjoy evading duty without having to pay the price for so doing, we are, the vast majority of us, on the side of law and society; and we recognize, perhaps ruefully, that you cannot get away with it for ever, that holidays are holidays only because they end, that mankind has after all to toe the line, and that duty has the last word.

I will not say anything in my own words on satire, which can certainly occur in plays bearing the name of comedies, because I do not find any satiric elements in Shakespeare's Comedies. Yet, as I am here being general, something should be said about satire. I cannot do better than quote L. J. Potts's remarks on how satire differs from comedy:

> Comedy and satire cannot in the last analysis be reconciled. The comic writer need not spare anything in nature, but he must not fall out with Nature herself. The satirist writes only from his own feelings; the comic writer must partly go outside his own feelings, to a conception of nature. . . . The distinction between them has something in common with the distinction between madness and sanity. . . . The madman is, and the satirist becomes for artistic purposes, purely subjective in standpoint. The sane man is more or less capable of mental detachment; and it is by his power of detachment, or his willingness to exercise it, that the comic writer is distinguished from the satirist. Great satirists are of course more than merely angry, bitter, or disappointed men; they are usually baffled idealists. They compare life as it is with life as they would have it be; and being unwilling or unable to reconcile the two, they attack that which is less dear to them.[1]

iii. ROMANCE

What makes Shakespearean comedy different from other great comedy is the admixture of the status of mind proper to romance; and by romance I mean the body

---

[1] Op. cit., p. 154.

of fairy lore, ballads, medieval narratives, Greek and Italian novels, and their great recent derivatives by Spenser and Sidney, which Shakespeare grew up with or got to know in maturity. Plenty has been written about this romantic background; but, as far as I know, not much about the motions of the mind to which it refers. Over so vast an area these are bound to be various but they agree in not trespassing on the mental area typical of comedy. Shakespeare's Comedies astonish because, at their best, they harmonize these two apparently alien areas. At its greatest romance can speak for a large group and touch Epic; but such manifestations, if they concern Shakespeare, are related to the Histories not the Comedies. I omit them here. The other strains of romance I am about to indicate are found in the Comedies in varying degrees.

Simple people have that in their minds that welcomes the marvellous even if the items that compose it fail to add up or to attain any further significance. Much of the romance matter available in Shakespeare's age played up to that instinct. A summary of the first incidents in *Huon of Bordeaux*, translated by Lord Berners and then popular, will illustrate sufficiently. Huon, having killed Charlot, Charlemagne's treacherous son, in self-defence, will be pardoned only if he submits to an ordeal; he must go to Babylon, enter the palace of the Admiral, Gaudya, kill the chief lord present, kiss the Admiral's daughter three times, bring back hawks, bears, youths, maidens, with a handful of hair from the Admiral's beard and four of his teeth. Setting out on his way to fulfil his ordeal, Huon visits Rome and Jerusalem, after which he meets a hermit, Gerames, who tells him of the two roads to Babylon, one longer and safer, the other shorter but traversing the realm of Oberon, with whom it is death to speak. Not answered, Oberon will stir up nature in the most terrifying way. Huon chooses the dangerous way. He enters a forest, and Oberon, wearing various magic accoutrements, meets him. After many days of trial Huon at last welcomes Oberon's hospitality whereupon Oberon is delighted and recounts how he is the son of Julius Caesar and the Lady of the Secret Isles, only three feet high because of the act of a jealous fairy but endowed by other fairies with all kinds of supernatural powers. And what follows is in keeping with these marvels. It is plain from this account that a main point, if not the main point, of *Huon* is the unfailing succession of fresh surprises.

Miss Bradbrook[1] writes of certain characters in Elizabethan comedy who 'embodied the simple dreams of the unlettered audience'. And these derive from the fairy tale. Many fairy tales are tales of dazzling success, like Cinderella's, and they minister to the innocent day-dreaming instinct of people whose way of life is hard and who enjoy imagining themselves the inheritors of happier and easier fortune. Nor would Shakespeare have found the fairy success-story only in the tales he heard orally at home; he would have found them in the collections of stories from the Italian. A good proportion of those in Painter's *Palace of Pleasure* are of this kind. Take, for instance, the thirty-fourth from the first book, derived from Boccaccio. Alexandro, nephew to three Florentine grandees of fluctuating fortunes, goes, when they fall on evil days, to seek his fortune in England. After some time there, it fell to his lot to accompany an abbot and his train on their journey from England to Rome. It turns out that the abbot is an English princess in disguise

[1] Op. cit., p. 78.

fleeing from an enforced marriage. She meets Alexandro, falls in love with him, and finally marries him. In his high prosperity he restores his uncles to their old fortune. Such stories belong to the mental realms of neither tragedy nor comedy. They do not concern man in society, being entirely self-centred, while the hero or heroine is too much at peace with himself and too much fortune's darling to approach the exaltations and agonies of the tragic protagonist.

But the success story need not be so simple or so dependent on mere luck. *Huon of Bordeaux* began with an ordeal but failed to make it significant; yet not all romance need fail in this way. If the ordeal tests character and not merely luck, it may open up important areas of the mind. In a primitive context it will suggest the act of growing up, the passage from boyhood to manhood and the need to prove through ceremonies of initiation that you are worthy so to pass. In an Elizabethan context it would lead to the idea of 'nurture', on which was then put such a high value: or it could be stated in terms of the finding of self; the chief character or characters ending up more than their old selves, or, never having had any recognizable selves, now acquiring them. But the success story that includes an adequate ordeal need not be thus educative; it can stand for certain ordinary yet mature and fundamental experiences of which men have decided generally to approve: a sea-voyage, not without its difficulties, ending safely in port; a man's taking a neglected farm and after difficulties and hardships, making it fruitful; even a man's going out to do a good day's work and returning home in the evening to relax. These are the feelings that Disney unconsciously tapped in his *Snow-white* in picturing the seven dwarfs coming back from work and

romping with Snow-white in the evening and then, singing their catchy song, setting out to work in their mine
next day. Or you can find them, poignantly contrasted
with the duty to take part in violent but necessary strife,
in William Morris's *Message of the March Wind*, as in this
passage:

> For it beareth the message: 'Rise up on the morrow,
> And go on thy ways toward the doubt and the strife;
> Join hope to our hope and blend sorrow with sorrow,
> And seek for men's love in the short days of life.'
>
> But lo, the old inn, and the lights, and the fire,
> And the fiddler's old tune and the shuffling of feet;
> Soon for us shall be quiet and rest and desire,
> And to-morrow's uprising to deeds shall be sweet.

They are the feelings too that go with certain simple
adages, such as that effort is the parent of pleasure, that
you can't get something for nothing, that only the brave
deserve the fair. This last adage suggests another success
story through ordeal: that of courtship. Men have agreed
that this is a very proper process, though opinions differ
as to the right length and severity of it. Capture by pirates
was a popular, inherited ingredient of the love romance
in the age of Elizabeth. Shakespeare, who constantly
used the theme, preferred something less violent.

As mirrored in the romance, the mental areas indicated in the last paragraph are proper to the individual,
guides to individual conduct. But it is also true that the
man who heeds them is likely to respect the demands of
society. Thus there may be links between romance and
comedy.

In sum, romance has to do with parts of the mind pre-
valent in children or very simple people or with certain

simple and fundamental things common to us all. Unlike St Paul, Shakespeare did not put away childish things when he grew to manhood, for he never surrendered any possession of his mind; rather he allowed childish things to live in harmony with things adult and sophisticated. And it is in the Comedies above all that he combines and harmonizes both kinds. This feat no other dramatist has achieved with anywhere near the same success. By achieving it he became a great popular dramatist and the dramatist whose comedies have the widest range. If you want a comparison with the wealth and the range of Shakespeare's comedies you must seek it not in other men's plays but in the *Odyssey* of Homer.

EDITOR'S NOTE TO CHAPTER II

The author inserted the following memorandum in the manuscript after its completion:

In writing on separate plays I may have got too far away from my talk on literary kinds. I must revise bearing in mind the different states of mind to be expected in Shakespearean comedy. They are these:

Comic proper

Man's relations with his neighbour and society and his need to come to terms with them.
Subdivisions Positive: here is how to behave.
Negative: offender brought to heel.

Farce

End is laughter through incongruity, with object of giving mind a holiday.
Admits fantasy, which, heightened, touches romance.

Picaresque
  1. Sympathy with underdog.
  2. Rebellion against duty; Anti-comedy.

Romance
  1. Enjoyment of marvellous (in simplest form primitive and inorganic).
  2. Success-story ministering to day-dream.
     (*a*) Dependent on luck.
     (*b*) Dependent on ordeal. This leads on to
  3. Expression of belief in certain simple and fundamental human rhythms.

Chapter III

THE COMEDY OF ERRORS

i. ITS ORIGINALS

THE core of the *Comedy of Errors* is farce and it is derived from one play of Plautus and some scenes from another.[1] In the *Menaechmi* the motive of farce is the arrival in Epidamnus of a man, the identical twin brother of another man settled and married in the town. The incoming brother has been seeking his twin for many years in his own ship. Before the brothers meet and exchange news, a number of people in Epidamnus mistake one brother for another with various ludicrous results; and these results are the reason for the play's existence. The play is short and neat, and the farcical situations are well contrived. None of the characters excites our sympathy, nor does the play possess any other quality that might distract our attention from the purely farcical effect. Shakespeare appropriated the main motive and many of the details. For instance, his Adriana, wife of the established brother, is jealous in imitation of the wife of Menaechmus, while each wife has some cause for jealousy in the shape of a local courtesan. And if Menaechmus gives his Erotium a cloak and a gold chain Antipholus gives Erotium's opposite number a gold chain but no cloak. Both husbands are thought to be mad by their wives and incur or escape capture with a view to the proper medical treatment. So in a sense

---

[1] For an exhaustive account of the sources see T. W. Baldwin, op. cit., chap. XVIII.

THE COMEDY OF ERRORS

Shakespeare got the core of his *Errors* from the *Menaechmi*.

But he was not at all strictly bound to his original. Indeed, in his youthful ambition, he was not satisfied till he had added so much to the Plautine core as to make his version a totally different affair.

First, he went to another play of Plautus, the *Amphitryo*, for help in complicating the farcical situation. In the *Menaechmi* only the incoming brother has his confidential slave; but in the *Amphitryo* not only does Jupiter assume Amphitryo's form to promote his intrigue with Alcmena but he causes Mercury to take the form of Sosia, Amphitryo's slave, thus creating two pairs, masters and servants, of identical appearance. Shakespeare imitated this creation by adding to the identical brothers identical brothers' servants. He also borrowed from the *Amphitryo* the farcical situation of a citizen being barred out of his own house by his wife. By adding this second pair of twins Shakespeare embarked on a much more complicated task than Plautus had attempted, as it were choosing to play chess as against Plautus's draughts. The range of possible mistakes was greatly extended; and Shakespeare was able to set his prodigious powers of memory and intellect a satisfyingly exacting task.

But Shakespeare also went outside Plautus to enrich his theme. However stylized and matter-of-fact Roman comedy was, it retained some faint trace of its more romantic ancestry through its motives of recognitions of lost children, its closeness to the sea, its allusions to shipwreck and pirates. It thus connects remotely with the Greek novel, which had a common origin with Latin comedy however widely it diverged from it. Shakespeare exploited this connection by enclosing his Plautine farce

47

in a framework derived from the Greek novel. In the *Menaechmi* the parents of the twin brothers figure among the characters; but they live in the town where the action takes place: and of the whole family it is only the second brother who does the travelling and the seeking. Moreover his travels are barely referred to. Shakespeare caused the parents to be separated, placing the father and one son in Syracuse and making them both search the world for the rest, who are living in the town where the action takes place, the mother as Abbess of a nunnery and the son a prosperous married citizen. And Shakespeare chose to recount both the events that led to the family's dispersal and the action of one separated part in seeking out the other. For this narrative he got his hints from the lost Greek romance of Apollonius of Tyre,[1] preserved in a Latin translation and retold by Gower. That Shakespeare read Gower's version is shown by his own dramatization of Apollonius's story, *Pericles*, with Gower speaking the prologue of each act. In the story a father seeks and finds a lost wife and daughter, the wife being priestess in the temple of Diana at Ephesus. It was this last detail that caused Shakespeare to change the Plautine setting of Epidamnus to Ephesus. Yet he had another reason to welcome this change. A crucial motive in the *Comedy of Errors* is that of the fairy world and especially witchcraft; and Shakespeare's audience, bred on the Bible, knew that Ephesus was noted for its magic arts. In the nineteenth chapter of the *Acts of the Apostles* it is recounted that 'certain of the vagabond Jews, exorcists, tried unsuccessfully to compete with St Paul in the expulsion of evil spirits, with the results that many Ephesians who

---

[1] He may have got hints from Greene's pastoral romance, *Menaphon*. See Baldwin, op. cit., p. 794. But Shakespeare's sobriety is unlike Greene's froth.

practised magic brought their handbooks to be burnt in
public. Thus Shakespeare added to the farcical nucleus
further examples of recognition after many years, episodes
of storms, shipwrecks, rescues, separations, and hints of
magical practice, all endemic in the world of romance.

Finally, Shakespeare did something which we need
not connect with any precedent. He humanized his
farcical nucleus and approximated it to comedy in a way
Plautus never even began to do. First, he made his
Ephesus a more living city than Plautus's Epidamnus.
Ephesus became a place where not only ridiculous things
happened but where men encountered the perennial
problem of how to live together in a society. Second, he
defined and contrasted his persons in a way Plautus never
tried to do. His two brothers are quite different in temperament; to the citizen-brother's wife he added a sister,
as different from her sister as he made brother from
brother; father and mother differ somewhat as brother and
brother do.

ii. RHETORIC

As the content of the *Comedy of Errors* is far more varied
than is often allowed, so is the vehicle. In the main, blank
verse prevails; but in the scenes where the low characters
figure there can occur prose, after the fashion of Lyly,
or four-stress doggerel after the fashion of *Ralph Roister
Doister* and of much comic stuff in the primitive Elizabethan drama. The scene of Antipholus of Ephesus along
with his Dromio bringing the Goldsmith and Balthazar
back home to dine and being barred out of his own
house begins with Antipholus talking in blank verse and
goes on to Dromio's replying in doggerel, with doggerel
continuing throughout this broadly comic episode, till

Balthazar turns to stately blank verse in his efforts to dissuade Antipholus from the scandal of breaking in at this busy time of day when half Ephesus may see him. The next scene, showing the other Antipholus courting Luciana and her attempts to reprove him, is in rhymed quatrains which suggest partly a sonneteering context, apt to the courting, and partly a sententious one, apt to Luciana's moralizing. Its rhetoric is perfectly fitting. But, if Shakespeare varies his blank verse with prose or other metres, that verse is more varied than it is reputed to be. True, it is largely end-stopped but within such a norm he can be extremely expressive; though only to an ear that is both attentive and unprejudiced. Take this example, from the opening scene, where Aegeon in calm and unhurried despair begins his tale of misfortunes:

> In Syracusa was I born, and wed
> Unto a woman, happy but for me,
> And by me, had not our hap been bad.
>
> (I, i, 37)

Here not only does the verse depart from its end-stopped context, but the third line is unusual and most expressive in rhythm. It must be read: And by me, had not our háp been bad, with *had* bearing a lighter stress than the other stressed words. Read thus, it suggests an afterthought following a long pause and serves to set up that feeling of the speaker's taking his time which is essential if we are to prepare ourselves for a long narrative. Or take the delicate adjustment of sound to sense in these two end-stopped lines (II, ii, 30–1):

> When the sun shines let foolish gnats make sport,
> But creep in crannies when he hides his beams.

Here the first line sounds gay and airy, the second low and earthy. And in final illustration, here is a passage end-stopped indeed yet so varied within its line-units as to give a sense of the most lively conversation. The context (IV, i, 52) is of the merchant to whom Angelo, the goldsmith, owes money, urging him to get from Antipholus of Ephesus his just debt for the chain.

Mer.   The hour steals on; I pray you, sir, dispatch.
Ang.   You hear how he importunes me—the chain!
Ant. E.   Why, give it to my wife, and fetch your money.
Ang.   Come, come, you know I gave it you even now.
          Either send the chain or send by me some token.
Ant. E.   Fie, now you run this humour out of breath!
          Come, where's the chain? I pray you let me see it.

Then there are the passages that, by sheer poetic eminence, are exceptions to the usual norm of metrical competence and aptitude. Take these few lines of soliloquy (I, ii, 33–8) spoken by Antipholus of Syracuse after the merchant has 'commended him to his own content' and left him:

He that commends me to mine own content
Commends me to the thing I cannot get.
I to the world am like a drop of water
That in the ocean seeks another drop,
Who, falling there to find his fellow forth,
Unseen, inquisitive, confounds himself.

Here there is not only the slow melancholy cadence that confirms the sentiment but the surprising collocation of *unseen* and *inquisitive*. Normally the inquisitive person does not worry whether he is seen or not. But Antipholus feels all the loneliness of a stranger at large in an alien city in which he is about to 'lose himself and wander up and down to view' it. Yet it is his duty to be inquisitive, and the surprising collocation of the two adjectives expresses both that duty and his despair of ever fulfilling it. It is a pleasant irony that as soon as he finishes his soliloquy he should cease to be unseen through being accosted by Dromio of Ephesus and prevented for good from taking his intended lonely walk round the town.

Then at the end of the same scene Shakespeare gives us a taste of his superb range of diction in Antipholus's account of what to expect in Ephesus:

> They say this town is full of cozenage;
> As, nimble jugglers that deceive the eye,
> Dark-working sorcerers that change the mind,
> Soul-killing witches that deform the body,
> Disguised cheaters, prating mountebanks,
> And many such-like liberties of sin;
>
> (I, ii, 97)

And the passage is matched by the other Antipholus's account of Pinch, the quack called in to treat him in his supposed madness. It is part of Antipholus's long appeal to the Duke to redress his wrongs (V, i, 237-41).

> Along with them
> They brought one Pinch, a hungry lean-fac'd villain,
> A mere anatomy, a mountebank,
> A threadbare juggler, and a fortune-teller,
> A needy, hollow-ey'd, sharp-looking wretch,
> A living dead man.

In sum, Shakespeare's rhetoric in the *Comedy of Errors* is good for something more than simple farce.

iii. THE ROMANTIC FRAMEWORK

In my short discussion of Shakespeare's originals I began

with the core of farce and worked outward. In going on to discuss the meaning of the different parts of the play I reverse this order, for I believe that it is in the core, as reinforced by the peripheries, that the main meaning of the play subsists.

In itself the romantic framework has no profound significance. It does not make us feel that either Aegeon or his younger son has surmounted an ordeal through the successful issue of his long wanderings; nor are we drawn anywhere near the feelings I have described as apt to the natural human routine of setting out from home, coping successfully with a task, and returning to relax. No, the romantic framework in itself does not go beyond arousing our simple feelings of wonder. Aegeon tells his story of marine adventures well enough, though not as well as Prospero was destined to tell his, and keeps our mind happily busy, yet not seriously extended, by its strangenesses. But in conjunction with the rest of the play the romantic framework weighs more. It helped to satisfy Shakespeare's craving for a rich subject-matter and in particular for an extreme complication of plot needing skilful disentanglement in the last scene. For the latter the added presence of Aegeon and Aemilia was essential. (Incidentally it is pleasant to reflect that not only does the first scene lead to the *Tempest* but the last scene to the grand finale of *Cymbeline*.) On the face of it, to graft remote romance on a crudely farcical plot was to court disaster; but it is precisely over such difficulties that Shakespeare was able to triumph. As it is, the fantasy of the romance leads easily to the fantastic shape which he caused the old farcical material to take on. When it comes to degrees of fantasy, there is nothing to choose between Aegeon and Aemilia tying one twin son and one twin slave to this

end of the mast and the other son and slave to that, and
Antipholus and Dromio of Syracuse going about Ephesus
with drawn swords convinced that they are surrounded
by witches and devils.

iv. THE COMIC ELEMENT

Here, in the play that may be his first comedy, we find
Shakespeare following what was to prove his permanent
instinct: never to forsake the norm of social life. However
distant he may get from that norm into inhuman horror,
or wild romance, or lyrical fancy, or mystical heights, he
always reverts, if only for a short spell, to the ordinary
world of men and to its problems of how they are to live
together. Even in the *Winter's Tale*, where the proportion
of the remote and the fantastic may be the highest,
Shakespeare recalls us to the gross life of ordinary folk
with the entry of the old shepherd and his 'I would there
were no age between ten and twenty-three' and the rest.
You may say that he was forced to do this to please his
public; but he was also following his instincts, which insisted on connecting, on demonstrating the unity of all
experience. It is an instinct that has made Shakespeare so
widely loved and the lack of which explains the com-
parative neglect of Spenser. The extent to which he in-
dulged that instinct in the *Comedy of Errors* has not been
fully recognized.

Take the setting. Though Henry Cuningham, in his
preface to the Arden *Errors*, may be right in identifying
the abbey in Ephesus with Holywell Priory near two of
the London playhouses, the Curtain and the Theatre,
Ephesus itself is a small ordinary town where everyone
knows everyone else's business, where merchants pre-

dominate, and where dinner is a serious matter. The last item suggests an illustration of how Shakespeare added normal life to farce. Though we hear plenty about Antipholus of Ephesus before, he does not appear on the stage till the beginning of the third act. But when he does his first words show we are in the very central area of comedy:

> Good Signior Angelo, you must excuse us all;
> My wife is shrewish when I keep not hours.
> Say that I linger'd with you at your shop
> To see the making of her carcanet,
> And that tomorrow you will bring it home.
>
> (III, i, 1)

Antipholus has indeed been laying up trouble for himself, for not only is he shockingly late for dinner but he is bringing with him two guests, probably unnotified and certainly offensive to the housewife as eating a dinner that through over-cooking does an injustice to her domestic competence. No wonder Antipholus tries to excuse himself on the ground that it was his solicitude for his wife's chain that made him late and seeks further safety by getting Angelo to father the lie. So, in their way, his sins are great, but how ludicrously different from the sins Adriana imputes to him. Or take a touch like this one. The second scene of the second act begins with Antipholus of Syracuse meeting his own Dromio and their immediately getting at cross purposes. Antipholus loses his temper and beats his slave; but his good nature asserts itself, and he tells Dromio to be more sensible and watch his master's mood before he talks nonsense to him.

> Because that I familiarly sometimes
> Do use you for my fool and chat with you,

55

Your sauciness will jest upon my love,
And make a common of my serious hours.
When the sun shines let foolish gnats make sport,
But creep in crannies when he hides his beams.
If you will jest with me, know my aspect,
And fashion your demeanour to my looks,
Or I will beat this method in your sconce.

(II, ii, 26)

Neither of these very human touches or the many others like them I could cite have any bearing on the purely farcical situations; but, as I shall explain, they may have a great deal of meaning if, not attempting to integrate comedy and farce, we set one in contrast to the other.

Then there are the characters. For the farcical effect, Shakespeare did not need to diversify them. Situations he must of course diversify even to extravagance; but the characters of those who find themselves in the situations hardly count. It would not matter if the two Antipholi were identical not only in appearance but in character. The primary need is that they should be subjected to a variety of accidents. But Shakespeare could not be content simply to satisfy this primary need; his nature insisted on his giving the two brothers different characters. The elder brother, Antipholus of Ephesus, is the more energetic, the more practical, the more choleric; the younger Antipholus is in comparison melancholy, sensitive, and of a livelier imagination. Barred from his house, Antipholus of Ephesus proposes to break in by force and has to be reminded by Balthazar of the scandal this would cause, before desisting. And after he has broken his bonds and escaped his confinement in the dark room he vows that he will scorch his wife's face and disfigure her. With his different temperament Antipholus of Syracuse

56

THE COMEDY OF ERRORS

is pessimistic about finding his brother, open to the notion that the Ephesians are queer folk and that there is witchcraft abroad, and slow in the practical matter of drawing the right conclusion from the way many people seem to know who he is and salute him. The contrast between the brothers is not thrust on us but it is there in all clarity, as it is there in *Cymbeline*, where, although the plot does not demand it, Shakespeare made Guiderius, the elder brother, the more practical and thrustful and Arviragus, the younger, more imaginative.[1] By distinguishing between the Antipholi in this way Shakespeare adds the comic to the purely farcical.

The parents, Aegeon and Aemilia, on the other hand, are hardly characterized at all. Aegeon is little more than a humour of aged melancholy; rightly, because, if fully animated, he would have introduced an element of tragedy that the farcical core could not have sustained. Aemilia, a symbol of severe and stately authority, but again hardly characterized, serves the play substantially. Her unexpected appearance (and we can picture her as tall and commanding, and conspicuous in her black habit among the excited particoloured folk that throng the stage) is one of the great moments of the play; an abrupt check to the wild fantasy that has been accumulating through the previous acts and a sign that the resolution is at hand. She is also the agent of the final drawing out of Adriana's character, when she 'betrays her to her own reproof'. Yet, though thus an agent of normal human action, she is hardly humanized herself.

It is on the two sisters that Shakespeare expends his power of making ordinary, living people. Bradley noted how few lines Cordelia speaks in comparison with the

[1] See my *Shakespeare's Last Plays* (London, 1938), p. 35.

impression she leaves behind. To a smaller extent this is true of Adriana and Luciana, to whose vivid characterization justice has hardly been done and whose natures, I venture to think, have not been properly understood. Shakespeare's study of the two sisters ranks, indeed, with other studies of that classic theme: with those found in the *Antigone*, *Arcadia*, the *Heart of Midlothian*, *Sense and Sensibility*, *Middlemarch*, and the *Old Wives' Tale*. In all these the sisters are different, sometimes opposed, in temperament, but loyal one to the other, however much their principles may differ and their actions in life diverge.

It is usual to describe Adriana as a jealous woman and to leave it at that. But this is too simple a description and indeed it heads us off the truth. It must be granted that she keeps on professing jealousy but her nature need not contain an excess of it. The root of her trouble is stupidity,[1] and lack of reflection and restraint that makes her her own worst enemy. She belongs to a higher rank in life than Mrs Quickly, but in her stupidity and her garrulousness she is like her. She is also good-natured at bottom and quick to forgive. All these qualities save the last are evident in the scene (II, i) in which she first appears. Here she is shown in distraction because her husband is late for dinner and Dromio, sent to fetch him, has not returned. And Luciana's sensible advice—

> Perhaps some merchant hath invited him,
> And from the mart he's somewhere gone to dinner;
> Good sister, let us dine, and never fret.
>
> (II, i, 4)

[1] It is surprising that E. P. Kuhl, who has written some of the sanest criticism on *The Shrew*, should call Adriana and Kate 'two mischief-making women—women much alike'. On the contrary Kate differs in being highly intelligent; and part of her education is for her to be made to use an intelligence overlaid by violent passions. See *P.M.L.A.*, 1925, pp. 611–12.

makes no impression on her. Finally, when Dromio returns and reports his supposed master's strange behaviour, she loses all restraint and acts the greatly injured wife. Sense in the shape of Luciana now reproves Sensibility only to receive (as Jane Austen caused her Elinor to receive) the accusation of emotional coldness: 'Unfeeling fools can with such wrongs dispense' (II, i, 103). The scene ends with Luciana's exclamation, 'How many fond fools serve mad jealousy!' She knows that stupidity is the root of the trouble. In the next scene, when the wrong Antipholus appears, Adriana lets him have the torrent of her complaint, once the supposed husband shows himself willing to enter the house for dinner, she cools rapidly:

> Come, come, no longer will I be a fool,
> To put the finger in the eye and weep,
> Whilst man and master laughs my woes to scorn.
> Come, sir, to dinner. Dromio, keep the gate.
> Husband, I'll dine above with you today,
> And shrive you of a thousand idle pranks.
>
> (II, ii, 202)

Alas, her resolution not to be a fool does not hold, and she has to pay the price. There is pathos in her relations with her husband; for when it comes to the point he trusts her, and we never doubt that in all practical matters she was an excellent wife. Thus, when he is in trouble he shouts to one of the Dromios:

> To Adriana, villain, hie thee straight;
> Give her this key, and tell her in the desk
> That's cover'd o'er with Turkish tapestry
> There is a purse of ducats; let her send it.
>
> (IV, i, 103)

But the stupid woman will not see that her husband is duly

59

dependent on her and that she can afford to leave him alone.
And so her creator sees to it that she is punished for her
stupidity. He makes the Lady Abbess the instrument.
Thinking her husband to be mad, Adriana tries to force
an entry into the abbey where he appears to have gone for
refuge, for she is convinced that only she can nurse him
back to health. The Abbess appears and wants to know
what is the matter with her refugee. Adriana, unaware of
the trap that is being laid for her, plunges headlong into
its recesses.[1]

> *Abb.* Hath he not lost much wealth by wreck of sea?
> Buried some dear friend? Hath not else his eye
> Stray'd his affection in unlawful love?
> A sin prevailing much in youthful men
> Who give their eyes the liberty of gazing.
> Which of these sorrows is he subject to?
> *Adr.* To none of these, except it be the last;
> Namely, some love that drew him oft from home.
> *Abb.* You should for that have reprehended him.
> *Adr.* Why, so I did.
> *Abb.*   Ay, but not rough enough.
> *Adr.* As roughly as my modesty would let me.
> *Abb.* Haply in private.
> *Adr.*   And in assemblies too.
> *Abb.* Ay, but not enough.
> *Adr.* It was the copy of our conference.
> In bed, he slept not for my urging it;
> At board, he fed not for my urging it;
> Alone, it was the subject of my theme;
> In company, I often glanced at it;
> Still did I tell him it was vile and bad.
> *Abb.* And thereof came it that the man was mad.

---

[1] In the light of this scene I just fail to see how Charles Brooks in
Shakespeare Quarterly (1960), p. 351 can say, 'Both Adriana and Kate are
admirably intelligent women.'

THE COMEDY OF ERRORS

> The venom clamours of a jealous woman
> Poisons more deadly than a mad dog's tooth.
>
> (V, i, 49)

And the Abbess spends sixteen more lines in rubbing this truth in. Whereupon Luciana can stand her silly sister's humiliation no longer but breaks in with

> She never reprehended him but mildly,
> When he demean'd himself rough, rude, and wildly.
> Why bear you these rebukes, and answer not?
>
> (V, i, 87)

The critics have gone wrong over Luciana even more than over Adriana, and with less excuse. C. H. Herford in his introduction to the play in the Eversley edition writes, 'Luciana brings us altogether into the atmosphere of lyric love'; Charlton calls her 'a gentle-hearted girl'; and Pettet talks of her 'romantic love story'. *Good-natured*, yes, witness the forbearing and tactful way she deals with her maddening sister; but *gentle-hearted*, no: that swerves in the wrong direction, for Luciana is essentially resolute in character. And as for *lyrical* and *romantic*, these epithets are quite alien to this shrewd and practical young woman. Luciana is what D. H. Lawrence called a 'hen-sure' woman; and nothing could be less romantic than her advice to Antipholus of Syracuse, when, mistaken for her brother-in-law, he makes love to her. It is pure wordly wisdom, tempered by a loyal solicitude for her sister's happiness.

> If you did wed my sister for her wealth,
> Then for her wealth's sake use her with more kindness
> Or, if you like elsewhere, do it by stealth;
> Muffle your false love with some show of blindness;

'Tis double wrong to truant with your bed
And let her read it in thy looks at board;
Shame hath a bastard fame, well managed;
Ill deeds is doubled with an evil word.

Then, gentle brother, get you in again;
Comfort my sister, cheer her, call her wife.
'Tis holy sport to be a little vain
When the sweet breath of flattery conquers strife.
(III, ii, 5–9, 17–20, 25–29)

Unlike her blundering sister, Luciana is observant. In
her loyalty she tells Adriana of Antipholus's advances
(IV, ii). Though shocked at their impropriety, she takes
note of their nature and admits that, addressed to the
proper person, they would be in very good style. In
another place her observant nature is conveyed with a
subtlety that few readers would expect of Shakespeare in
so early a play. In II, ii, Adriana and Luciana, mistaking
one Antipholus for the other, try to persuade Antipholus
of Syracuse to enter the house and eat the long-postponed
dinner. Utterly bewildered, he allowed himself to be
persuaded and tells us so in an aside. Whereupon Luciana
cries out, 'Dromio, go bid the servants spread for dinner.'
She has heard nothing, but she has been watching Antipholus's face and sees that he has changed his former mind.

To anthologize and isolate such examples of character-
building incurs the risk of making them too prominent.
Therefore, as a safeguard, let it be remembered that they
ever remain subordinate to the main farcical business.

v. THE FARCICAL CORE

Not only did Shakespeare diversify farce by adding romance and comedy but he added delight and meaning to

his farce by sharpening its elements and by taking farce beyond itself.

First, he subjects his brothers to different trials and adjusts their states of mind accordingly. Antipholus of Ephesus suffers a number of indignities and takes them seriously, at their face value. To an actor commanding a wide range of grim facial expressions he offers a superb part. And incongruity between the grim expression and the ultimately trivial nature of the things that cause it will be the main and most sufficient cause for laughter. The case of Antipholus of Syracuse is different and has not been fully understood. This Antipholus does not suffer in-dignities. On the contrary he is fortune's favourite; but he cannot relish her favours because he thinks they are illusory. The final states of mind of the brothers are alike in being strange, but in every other way they are sharply, and of course deliberately, contrasted. It is worth describing the progress of the younger Antipholus's state of mind as subjected to one benefit after another, until the sequence at last breaks and we know the end is near.

We first see Antipholus of Syracuse in the company of a friendly merchant, who has warned him to profess to come from Epidamnus (or Epidamium, as Shakespeare calls it) so as to avoid the law against the Syracusans that Aegeon has just run into. That is a good piece of luck. Next he thinks that something has happened to his money, which he ordered his Dromio to lay up in safety at his inn. And this misapprehension brings to mind the reputa-tion of Ephesus as a city of swindlers and magicians and precipitates his soliloquy on the theme, already quoted as an example of some of the best poetry the play contains. The soliloquy comes at a most emphatic place, the end of

63

the first act, and shows its deliverer ready to believe anything about the town at which he has arrived. Having
visited his inn, Antipholus of Syracuse finds that his money
is safe after all; but his reassurance is quickly dispelled by
his being assailed by an unknown woman who claims him
for her husband and forces him to enter her house. His
perplexities recur, and Dromio has now no doubt of the
enchantment that surrounds them:

> This is fairyland. O spite of spites!
> We talk with goblins, owls, and sprites.
> If we obey them not, this will ensue:
> They'll suck our breath, or pinch us black and blue.
>
> (II, ii, 188)

Yet in all this Antipholus is a gainer, for he enjoys a
good dinner for nothing and the company of a girl with
whom he at once falls in love. But the girl thinks him
mad and tries to divert his advances, and when his
Dromio gives his fantastic account of the spherical
kitchen-maid who claims him, haunts him, and would
have him he concludes, 'There's none but witches do
inhabit here', and decides that the charmer is a mermaid,
and that they must get out of Ephesus as quickly as
possible. (Note that while Antipholus pursues Luciana,
Dromio flies in terror from the kitchen-maid.) But before
he can decamp, an unknown man enters and thrusts on
him the gift of a gold chain: the kind of thing that might
happen in a fairy romance.

And here I must digress about the use Shakespeare
makes of gold, which is very frequently mentioned in
the play. The motive of the gold chain, which is prominent
in the plot, first enters at the end of the first scene of act
two. Here Adriana tells her sister that her husband has

promised her the gold chain. She then proceeds to moralize about gold in lines which unfortunately are corrupt and have not been explained satisfactorily. In spite of corruption it is at least clear that gold is solid and will stand up to rubbing in a way that mere surface enamel will not:

> I see the jewel best enamelled
> Will lose his beauty; yet the gold bides still
> That others touch
>
> (II, i, 109)

(Here *jewel* means not precious stone but piece of jewelry.) But the gold chain behaves in a way alien to the solidity of the material from which it is fashioned. It eludes its true owner, it leads to all kinds of mistakes, and the man to whom it is given in error enjoys it as one of a number of things of whose existence he is doubtful. In fact, though Antipholus does not actually state it, the chain for him is fairy-gold and might wither away to nothing at any moment. No sooner has the wrong Antipholus got the chain than (IV, i) we see a merchant pressing the goldsmith for a debt, and the goldsmith promising to fulfil it through the money Antipholus of Ephesus is about to give him for the chain. To them comes Antipholus in high fettle after his dinner with the courtesan and full of vengeful feelings against his household that have barred him out of his house. His first words, before he sees the goldsmith, are to his Dromio:

> While I go to the goldsmith's house, go thou
> And buy a rope's end, that will I bestow
> Among my wife and her confederates,
> For locking me out of my doors by day.
>
> (IV, i, 15)

The rope is the substitute for the chain he would have

given, had his wife behaved herself. But it is more than that, for it was no accident that the rope enters the play in a context of gold. As gold keeps on attaching itself to Antipholus of Syracuse, so ropes attach themselves, metaphorically and literally, to Antipholus of Ephesus. As the latter fails to get the chain that belongs to him and later the gold that should set him free from bonds, so does he get the rope's end he has ordered and must submit to be bound by ropes in a way he had not bargained for. In fact, gold and rope are contrasted symbols of what the two brothers experience; and there is a delightful irony in the younger brother's distrusting the first, and the elder brother's not welcoming the second.

To revert to the fortunes of Antipholus of Syracuse. As the day wears on, he becomes more and more bewildered:

> There's not a man I meet but doth salute me
> As if I were their well-acquainted friend;
> And every one doth call me by my name.
> Some tender money to me, some invite me,
> Some other give me thanks for kindnesses,
> Some offer me commodities to buy;
> Even now a tailor call'd me in his shop,
> And showed me silks that he had bought for me,
> And therewithal took measure of my body.
> Sure, these are but imaginary wiles,
> And Lapland sorcerers inhabit here.
>
> (IV, iii, 1)

And—final stroke of unappreciated good fortune—his Dromio brings him the gold intended to ransom his arrested brother. And now, so far has he acquiesced in the belief that all is illusion, he does not beat his Dromio for being drunk and making inept jokes but infers that he too suffers from the prevailing enchantment:

> The fellow is distract, and so am I;
> And here we wander in illusions.
> Some blessed power deliver us from hence!
>
> (IV. iii, 37)

From this point on Antipholus of Syracuse ceases to be fortune's favourite and has to defend himself; also he not only thinks others to be enchanters but is thought by others to be mad. He thus approaches, rather than is thought different from, his brother. The change begins when, immediately after the speech just quoted, the courtesan enters and sees him wearing the chain that the other brother had promised her. She claims it, and he thinks she is the devil in human form and seeks to drive her away. Although there is no stage direction, surely Antipholus of Syracuse draws his sword to drive away the supposed witch, in preparation for his next and culminating entry. Remaining behind, the courtesan says that he must be mad. The culminating entry is when, just after Adriana and various others have seen Antipholus of Ephesus bound and haled away to be treated as a madman, the other brother and his Dromio enter with drawn swords; whereupon all those on the stage think that the madman has broken loose and disperse in panic. Antipholus of Syracuse remarks that the witches are afraid of swords; but by now he is quite unnerved and vows that he 'will not stay tonight for all the town'. But more trouble awaits him, for he encounters the goldsmith and the merchant, who demand money for the chain he is still wearing. A fight threatens but is averted by Dromio's dragging his master into the neighbouring priory for asylum. So end the trials of Antipholus of Syracuse.

In his excellent edition of the *Comedy of Errors*[1] (excellent, that is, for the mature scholar but well calculated to depress the school-boy, for whom it is supposed to cater) T. W. Baldwin rightly says that a main interest of the play is 'the intellectual ingenuity Shakespeare has displayed in managing to continue to get the wrong persons together at exactly the right time to keep the confusions constantly increasing'. There is indeed something massive about the intellectual power Shakespeare here displays: a power of holding in suspense in the mind a vast quantity of detail and of being able to call on any item in it at the shortest notice. A good example of this power occurs at the end. All has been disclosed; our minds are occupied solely with the main farcical themes; and the whole company enter the priory except the two pairs of twins. Shakespeare has not forgotten (what the spectator or reader at this point surely has) that the twins are still indistinguishable and that though one Dromio will know the other Dromio he will not know the right Antipholus. So he makes Dromio of Syracuse ask the wrong Antipholus, 'Master, shall I fetch your stuff from shipboard?' (V, i, 407) and thereby takes us back to the two happenings: first, Dromio's taking his master's luggage on board ship in preparation for flight from the wizardries of Ephesus, and second his reporting that he has done so to the wrong brother. And when, their masters having gone in, the two Dromios are left together on the stage, they pass no comments on the strangeness of it all, as a lesser dramatist would have made them do. Instead, Shakespeare reverts to a second forgotten theme: the monstrous kitchen-maid. She still haunts the mind of Dromio of Syracuse; but now it occurs to him that she can

[1] Boston, Mass., 1928, p. xxxii.

be exorcized, for she is his brother's responsibility. So he says (*sister* of course meaning *sister-in-law*):

> There is a fat friend at your master's house,
> That kitchen'd me for you today at dinner;
> She now shall be my sister, not my wife.

$$(V, i, 413)$$

(How Shakespeare could remember if he was interested! and how he could forget if he was not! Plainly dates bored him, for the chronology in the play is shocking.) It was through this power of holding all the items in suspense till the end that Shakespeare was able to delight the reader by springing on him this double surprise.

In remembering the intellectual charm of the *Comedy of Errors* we must not forget its sheer power of diverting a mixed audience and taking it out of itself. Granted that by some device the simplest among the spectators could know at once which Antipholus or Dromio was on the stage, the play progresses successfully from one hilarity to an ever wilder one, fulfilling superbly the basic function of a farce.

When an example of a lesser literary kind reaches a certain pitch of excellence it is apt to transcend the kind to which it belongs. And, if we are to perceive what the *Comedy of Errors* succeeds at last in doing, we should do well to consider high specimens of farce. Take first Chaucer's *Miller's Tale*. Although this approaches comedy, the central plots are farcical, the supreme farcical moment being when Nicholas, the victim in one part of the plot, calls for water to ease his scorched buttocks and by so calling makes the carpenter, the victim in the other part of the plot, think that the flood has happened and cut the rope that holds up his boat. I have pleaded in my *Poetry Direct*

69

and Oblique[1] that in the *Miller's Tale*, and especially at the supreme moment, Chaucer touches an area of the mind outside the area to which farce belongs. But Chaucer's tale is fairly simple, and I refer to it for the above general reason and not because it is much like the *Comedy of Errors*. Nearer to the *Comedy* are some of René Clair's films, particularly *Belles de Nuit* and the early films (*Les Deux Timides* for instance) founded on farces of Labiche. Like the usual run of farces, these begin in ordinary life; they then turn ordinary life into something fantastic and remote from life; and then somehow they seem to rejoin life, but at a different point, so that, instead of making us feel what an amusing holiday from life this is, they cause us to exclaim, 'Oh but life after all can be as strange as all this.'

In my book on Shakespeare's last plays I had as one of my themes what I called 'planes of reality'. Of course I should not dream now of using such a phrase, for since 1938 'levels' have driven out 'planes' just as 'approaches' have driven out 'avenues'. What I meant was that for different people and for the same people at different times the norm of reality is not the same; and I may as well quote a few sentences from my book[2] to explain myself:

Most people get a sense of pleasant and reassuring solidity from their everyday occupations. If their nerves are in good order, they find such acts as buying writing-paper, catching a train, or answering an invitation, to be parts of a substantial core of existence. Virginia Woolf has summed up this state of things with perfect vividness and conciseness in the words, 'Tuesday follows Monday'. . . . It cannot be doubted that Shakespeare, with his eye for detail and his healthily slow development, fully shared this way of feeling. . . . There are, however, times when in the realm

---

[1] London, 1945, pp. 85–92.   [2] pp. 60–8.

of action even the simplest and the most normal people find their scale of reality upset. Under the stress of war, or love, or remorse, or a strong disappointment, the things that seemed solid, the acts that seemed to proceed so naturally and without question from one's will, appear remote. Eating and buying writing-paper become rather ridiculous acts which you watch yourself, or rather yourself appearing not your self, proceeding to do. . . . Once the equipoise is disturbed, the real things are not everyday acts but passionate mental activities. . . . No great poet can be unaware of these and other planes of reality, and in one way or another he has to make his peace with them. . . . The normal poetic method of dealing with them is to try to unite them by referring to a single norm; but there is another method: that of communicating the sense of their existence without arranging them in any pattern of subordination.

And I cite *A Midsummer Night's Dream* as an example of the first method, everything in the end being subordinated to the comic, social, norm; and *The Waves* as an example of the second.

In transcending mere farce as I think it to do, the *Comedy of Errors* raises the question of what is the norm of reality. One need not suppose that, at any rate at this stage of his career, Shakespeare had consciously formulated any opinions on such matters; but it is certain that he was aware of many modes or standards of experience well before he came to write his play; and what literary kind more than farce, with its congenital bent to the fantastic, was likely to express that awareness? I have said what I think to be the culminating moment of the play: namely when Antipholus of Syracuse and his Dromio enter with drawn swords, and Adriana and the rest think them her husband and servant broken loose and fly in terror. Both parties suffer from an extremity of illusion, one as it were ratifying the illusion of the other. Moreover the states of mind have been arrived at by gradual and entirely logical processes. And we conclude that the state of violence presented has somehow acquired its own solidity and thus stands for a way of experiencing, alternative to the way common in the plain working world.

On the whole things go right in the *Comedy of Errors*. The pathos of Aegeon in the last scene, when his younger son apparently refuses to recognize him, is too turgid to carry conviction:

> Though now this grained face of mine be hid
> In sap-consuming winter's drizzled snow,
> And all the conduits of my blood froze up,
> Yet hath my night of life some memory,
> My wasting lamps some fading glimmer left,
> (V, i, 310)

(But note how the last line frees itself from the turgid and carries conviction.) The backchat in II, ii, between Antipholus of Syracuse and his Dromio is excessively dreary to a modern, however pleasing the word-play was in its time. But these are mere details and are exceptions. It is worth noting here that Dromio of Syracuse's account of the kitchenmaid in III, ii, succeeds by modern as well as by contemporary taste. It is as near to us as a music-hall turn and builds up a convincing picture of a monster. Having built it up, Shakespeare was wise not to bring her on the stage but to trust to our imaginations. Ignoring the blemishes, I find that the play is about as good as the verse allows. The verse has its limits and probably would not have reached to some subtle development of character, for instance. But it reaches to the things attempted; and the play has not been rated a major success only because it is Shakespeare's.

Chapter IV

THE TAMING OF THE SHREW

i. INITIAL DIFFICULTIES

I F the *Comedy of Errors* has been underprized, it is because, as immature Shakespeare, it has not been read
closely enough. Few critics have sought to disintegrate
it, and readers have not been distracted by the thought that
perhaps this or that scene is not by Shakespeare. Even if
their reading has been rather superficial at least it has been
serene. With the *Taming of the Shrew* the case is different,
for it has been widely held that Shakespeare did not write
the parts of the play that have to do with the wooing of
Bianca. Such opinion may not now be preponderant, for it
is indeed hard to postulate double authorship for a play in
which the two plots are so constantly and firmly inter-
woven, but it has caused readers to accept too readily the
premiss on which the opinion was based, namely that the
Bianca portion is vastly inferior to the Katherina portion;[1]
with the result that, expecting little from the former, they
have found less than is actually there. The same process
has dictated the usual type of presentation on the stage.
The Bianca plot is pure comedy in the Classico-Italianate
manner; the Katherina plot is comedy with farcical elements and is derived from folk-themes capable of crude or
gross treatment. If you play down the Bianca plot or accept
it as a liability from which you would willingly escape, you
tend to miss the comic elements in the Katherina plot and

[1] Note as an exception Hardin Craig, *An Interpretation of Shakespeare*
(New York, 1948), pp. 95–6.

73

to exaggerate the farcical ones. Thus, most productions put everything into the more grotesque side of the Induction, that is the drunkenness of Sly, and the more boisterous of the passages between Petruchio and Katherina. It is natural enough for producers to behave in this way, for from an ordinary audience you will get a quicker return from the crudities of farce than from the delicacies of good comedy. Thus it happens that the current picture of the *Shrew*, whether derived from reading or theatre, is lopsided.

Not that we can be certain that the version of the play that we have, that is the unique version preserved in the First Folio, entirely represents Shakespeare's intentions. It is difficult to believe that at some stage his play did not include an epilogue on the lines of that preserved in the *Taming of a Shrew*; and it is likely that some parts were written at a later date than others. Few readers do not feel an abrupt change of style when the play proper follows the Induction. There is no need to jump to the conclusion that here is proof of a different hand, for to begin a play within in exactly the same style as that of its enclosing agent would be gross dramatic incompetence; Shakespeare was forced to differentiate. Nevertheless the difference is such as to suggest that he did not write both at the same time, the Induction being rather more mature. And then there are the signs of a carelessness that exceeds the norm of a dramatist more careful about big things than about small.[1] There is, for instance, the unmotivated appearance of Hortensio at Petruchio's country house just after he has renounced Bianca and decided to go for safety and the wealthy widow. These things may cause a slight

[1] The most convenient place for information on these is in the *New Cambridge Shakespeare*, p. 124 ff.

uneasiness and make us wish that we had a better version than that preserved in the First Folio, but they are trivial compared with the distortion brought about by neglecting the Bianca plot.

The simplest way to point out the quality that the Bianca plot can touch is through an illustration. I choose the last lines of Act IV Scene iv. The scene is staged before Lucentio's lodging and it mainly presents the Pedant in his impersonation of Vincentio discussing with Baptista the arrangements for the marriage between Lucentio and Bianca. Baptista agrees that these should take their proper legal shape, and Tranio, impersonating Lucentio, asks where the proceedings shall take place. Baptista answers

> Not in my house, Lucentio, for you know
> Pitchers have ears, and I have many servants;
>
> (IV, iv, 51)

Tranio then suggests his own lodging, and after Cambio (the real Lucentio) has been ordered to warn Bianca of what has been settled and Biondello to fetch a scrivener, Baptista, Tranio, and the Pedant enter Lucentio's lodging, leaving Lucentio and Biondello on the stage. Then follows the dialogue I have in mind. On it the *New Cambridge Shakespeare* has the following note:

> We suspect adaptation here. . . . Biondello's off-hand, not to say impertinent, manner with Lucentio-Cambio in the dialogue which follows suggests that the writer of the dialogue has forgotten Cambio's real identity. The boy calls him Cambio throughout.[1]

The Cambridge editors are right in pointing out the exceptional impertinence, but in casting doubts both on the

[1] I agree with the suggestion, in the same note, about the stage-directions of the Folio and the characters' movements on the stage.

integrity of the passage and on its being by the Master, they rob him of some of his most delightful comic strokes. Biondello (the fair-headed boy, as the name tells us), has been cheeky and precocious from the beginning (after the manner of Lyly's pages) and now makes the most of his culminating opportunity, never to be repeated, of being very impertinent indeed. Soon Cambio will have reverted to Lucentio and require a higher standard of respect. But now is Biondello's chance. Baptista, grave gentleman and in point of manners worthy of respectful imitation, has just called Lucentio Cambio; and Biondello has news so joyful and exciting that, however he delivers it, Lucentio will never have the leisure or inclination to take the delivery amiss. For the news is that everything is now in train for the clandestine wedding, and that Lucentio can go straight ahead. So Biondello can risk calling his master by his assumed servant's name, and deliver his message in a studiedly off-hand way. This is how it begins:

Bion. Cambio.
Luc. What say'st thou, Biondello?
Bion. You saw my master wink and laugh upon you?
Luc. Biondello, what of that?
Bion. Faith, nothing; but has left me here behind to expound the meaning or moral of his signs and tokens.
Luc. I pray thee moralize them.
Bion. Then thus: Baptista is safe, talking with the deceiving father of a deceitful son.

(IV, iv, 73)

Biondello gets away with this piece of impertinence, for Lucentio ignores it and merely answers with, 'And what of him?' And the dialogue goes on:

Bion. His daughter is to be brought by you to the supper.

76

Luc. And then?

Bion. The old priest at Saint Luke's church is at your command at all hours.

Luc. And what of all this?

Bion. I cannot tell, except they are busied about a counterfeit assurance. Take *you* assurance of *her*, cum privilegio ad imprimendum solum; To th' church! take the priest, clerk, and some sufficient honest witnesses:

(IV, iv, 83)*

And Biondello proceeds to cap his references to marriage in terms of printing and copyright with a couplet of doggerel, a metre used for the more trivial parts of the comedy:

If this be not that you look for, I have no more to say,
But bid Bianca farewell for ever and a day.

(IV, iv, 92)

That completes Biondello's message; but Lucentio, the anxious lover, has more questions to ask, and the dialogue goes on:

Luc. Hear'st thou, Biondello?

Bion. I cannot tarry. I knew a wench married in an afternoon as she went to the garden for parsley to stuff a rabbit;

And so may you, sir;

And so adieu, sir.

My master hath appointed me to go to Saint Luke's to bid the priest be ready to come against you come with your appendix.

(IV, iv, 94)

And Biondello vanishes before Lucentio can get in his intended question. I do not know the Elizabethan connotations of *appendix*; perhaps *hanger-on* is a rough modern equivalent. Anyhow it contradicts the romantic feelings that Lucentio may be expected to feel at this moment for his Bianca, as the comparison of himself to the maid going to the garden for parsley to stuff a rabbit punctures the natural self-satisfaction of the successful lover.

In its little way this dialogue could not be bettered; it is as good, on however smaller a scale, as the scene in Petruchio's house with the haberdasher and the tailor. And yet, just because it belongs to the Bianca plot, no one to my knowledge has noticed its excellence. And its excellence is perfectly dramatic: we can see Biondello dancing on the tips of his tocs as he chants,

> And so may you, sir;
> And so adieu, sir.

triumphant that he has used his moments of advantage to the full.

I am not wishing to inflate the Bianca plot into a grand affair but I hope that the excellence of the above short part of it shows that it has not been treated with sufficient care and sympathy.

The last difficulty I have to mention has to do with the Petruchio-Katherina plot. Here opinion is widely divided. Is that plot comic or farcical? Does it deal with ridiculous situations too remote from reality for human emotions to be relevant, or with real people and their problems of living together? The answers take us into the heart of the play and demand a separate section.

ii. COMEDY OR FARCE?

Mark Van Doren has no doubt about the answer to this question:

Petruchio is hero of a farce, not of a romance. Comedy is made

... from situation: a shrew is to be tamed, a man is found to tame her, and he proceeds to do so by as many devices as can be developed in the time available. The interest of the audience will be in the devices, not in the persons who work them or upon whom they are worked. A certain callousness will be induced to form in the sensibilities of the beholder, so that whereas in another case, he would be outraged he will now laugh freely and steadily for two hours.[1]

He cannot, however, allow things to remain as simple as that but adds that the abiding interest of the play consists in the stages through which for both main characters love replaces pride. It is hard to see how, once this process is posited, the characters can fail to usurp their share of the interest. Yet Van Doren explicitly denies any such happening:

> Our secret occupation as we watch *The Taming of the Shrew* consists of noting the stages by which both Petruchio and Katherine—both of them, for in spite of everything the business is mutual—surrender to the fact of their affection. Shakespeare has done this not by violating his form, not by forgetting at any point to write farce, and least of all by characterizing the couple. He has left them man and woman.

At the other end of the scale Nevill Coghill[2] is equally emphatic that the play is not a farce and that the Petruchio-Katherina business is clearly motivated:

> *The Taming of the Shrew* has often been read and acted as a wife-humiliating farce in which a brute fortune-hunter carries all, including his wife's spirit, before him, to the general but vicarious joy of hen-pecked husbands. Yet it is not so at all. True, it is based on the medieval conception of the obedience owed by a wife to her wedded lord, a conception generously and charmingly

---

[1] *Shakespeare* (New York, 1939), p. 48 ff.
[2] *Essays and Studies of the English Association* (1950), p. 10–11.

asserted by Katerina at the end. But it is a total misconception to suppose that she has been bludgeoned into it.

Further, Coghill considers Katherina's shrewishness not just 'given' but cunningly motivated:

> She is a girl of spirit, yet has to endure a father who has openly made a favourite of her sly younger sister, and who is willing, even more openly, to sell his daughters to the highest bidder. . . . Thus environed, what choice has Katerina but to show her disdainful temper if she is to keep her self-respect?

Petruchio, though a self-admitted fortune-hunter, is likeable: good-natured and candid, though loud-mouthed and swaggering. To Katherina he is the one escape from her horrible family.

> The defensive technique of shrewishness was no final solution of her troubles. It was too negative. Yet she had adopted it so long that it seemed to have become second nature to her. It is this which Petruchio is determined to break in her, not her spirit.

Both critics are right in that they could advance valid evidence for their opinions, and both are wrong in that they fail to take everything into account, thus making Shakespeare's play a tidier thing than in fact it is. Neither admit to what a total reading of the play insists on concluding: that, though in detail the *Shrew* may be even better than is usually thought, it remains in its chief outlines not quite consistent, not completely realized or worked out. As a whole it is a comedy on the theme of appearance and reality with the excellent social moral that you must always be careful to look below the surface. But the two plots have the air of having pre-existed and then having been chosen for juxtaposition to illustrate the theme; not of having grown naturally out of an already existent urge to exploit it. In the Petruchio-Katherina scenes the more primitive strain coexists with the more civilized one. The latter may preponderate, and Shakespeare may well have wished to get rid of the other altogether; but if so, he did not carry out his wishes: in part Petruchio remains the tamer of animals. Having embarked already on the 'taming' part of the play, I continue dealing with it, postponing the matter of how the two plots are related and into what they issue.

Accustomed as we now are to find more and more subtleties in Shakespeare, most of us are emotionally inclined to credit Petruchio with considerable delicacy and perceptiveness of feeling under his violent exterior and we shall meet abundant corroboration for being so inclined. It is also to the interest of the play that Petruchio should thus illustrate decisively the master theme of appearance and reality. Let me illustrate Petruchio's delicacy or perceptiveness. In the long courting scene (II, i), when Petruchio and Katherina have their contest of wits, Petruchio shows delicacy of feeling in giving her the chance of saving her face before the rest if she should change her tune and accept him quietly, for he says to Baptista, 'If she be curst, it is for policy', and follows this up with ''Tis bargained 'twixt us twain, being alone,/That she shall still be curst in company.' In the same context Petruchio keeps on referring to Katherina's beauty; and it may be legitimate to suppose that in so doing he adopts a policy towards her that her family had been foolish to omit. Then there are his reiterated suggestions of sharing; that they are really at one if only she would see it. His outrageous clothes at the wedding are an emblem that proclaims: these are to my true self what your own shrewishness is to your true self; and each as well as the other can change the assumed self for the true one. This is what Petruchio means when he says, just before the wedding, 'To me she's married, not unto my clothes'; and at once Tranio ratifies the emblematic quality of those clothes with, 'He hath some meaning in his mad attire.' And when after the wedding the taming begins in earnest, the sharing continues. If Katherina has a cold rough journey to the country house, so has Petruchio. If she is deprived of supper, so is he also. And he speaks of them jointly suffering choler:

> And better 'twere that both of us did fast,
> Since, of ourselves, ourselves are choleric,
> Than feed it with such over-roasted flesh . . .
> And for this night we'll fast for company.

$$(IV, i, 157)$$

And he shows much patience in bearing with her stupidity when she will not see the game he has been playing. If she could not recognize the game when Petruchio abuses the haberdasher over the cap, at least when he repeats the game with the tailor, she should have seen it and consented to join in. And when she insists on putting him right on the time of day, his patience in not abandoning the game is almost saintly.

The culminating scene (IV, v) when she either submits or cooperates deserves separate treatment. It opens with, Petruchio, Katherina, and Hortensio on their way back to Padua. Petruchio continues his game by calling the sun the moon, and Katherina prolongs her stupidity by contradicting him. Petruchio orders an about-turn and complains of being 'Evermore cross'd and cross'd, nothing but cross'd!' Whereupon, Hortensio whispers to her, 'Say as he says, or we shall never go'; and his words produce the complete *volte-face*. To all appearances, she has been worn down and submitted her own will to a stronger. And yet, directly after, enlightenment descends and she sees that Petruchio has been playing a game in which she is free to join; and join in she does. Of this there is no doubt. When Vincentio enters and, having saluted him as 'gentle mistress' Petruchio asks her whether she has beheld a fresher gentlewoman, she takes her cue and salutes Vincentio as such. Further, she follows Petruchio when he pretends to correct his error. What makes certain that she is not the blindly obedient animal whose spirit has been broken but the willing ally is that she puts her apology to Vincentio in terms of her final discord with Petruchio:

> Pardon, old father, my mistaking eyes,
> That have been so bedazzled with the sun
> That everything I look on seemeth green.
>
> (IV, v, 44)

Vincentio cannot understand the full import of the reference to the sun, for it is a secret between the pair who have suddenly reached mutual understanding. And not only does it convey a secret, it also apologizes for a state of blindness, long maintained and only just perceived. Hardin Craig,[1] Nevill Coghill, and J. R. Brown[2] are all right in making the passage bear a big weight of meaning. Craig's comment can be heartily accepted:

> Katharina has never seen herself as others see her. In order to make her aware of the true nature of her behavior Petruchio burlesques Katharina's unreasonable conduct, and thus shows her a picture of herself . . . She has always behaved like a fool, although she is not a fool, and her new sense of humor is an indication of a profound change within her.

I think we may even go as far as to find an analogy in Jane

[1] *An Interpretation of Shakespeare* (New York, 1948), p. 90.
[2] *Shakespeare and his Comedies* (London, 1957), pp. 94-7.

Austen's Emma, who, in spite of a very good brain, made a great fool of herself in promoting a match between Harriet Smith and Frank Churchill, until brought to her senses by finding that Harriet has made a mistake and thought that Knightley was the man. Once brought to her senses, she sizes up the situation with the utmost speed: 'Her own conduct, as well as her own heart, was before her in the same few minutes. She saw it all with a clearness which had never blessed her before.' These words might fairly be applied to Shakespeare's Katherina also. But all this psychological plausibility in her should not cause us to forget, as it appears to make Coghill and Brown forget, that it follows on a different, perhaps incompatible state of mind, that of the tamed animal.

The last scene of the play with Katherina's great speech on the subordination of wives readily accommodates itself to whatever notions we have acquired in the course of reading the play. It may display her as the dutiful slave of her wedded lord, repeating mechanically the lore he has imposed on her; it may display her, now a sensible social Elizabethan, uttering the commonplaces of conservative opinion of the age, much as Juliet and Portia were destined to do (Juliet's 'And all my fortunes at thy foot I lay/ And follow thee my lord throughout the world' is as extreme as anything in Katherina's speech); it may continue the game of acting a part which Katherina, her eyes once open, enjoys doing and does well, or, in Charles Brooks's[1] words, 'She plays her part so well that only she and Petruchio know how much is serious and how much put on.'

There is thus a great deal to be said for thinking Petruchio's way with Katherina civilized; and Hardin Craig is not bothered with the things that point the other

[1] Op. cit., p. 354.

way: 'Although the stupid wife-taming, through hunger and cruelty, of the source is preserved as the machinery of the plot, it has lost its essential quality.' I wish I could agree but I cannot; for though Van Doren is wrong in thinking you can be happy with the play as a farce, there remain parts which, tolerable in a farce, are incompatible with the civilized character of much of the rest.

First, it is useless to pretend that Petruchio used only the human oblique methods of parodying in his own excesses the excesses of Katherina and then letting her draw her conclusions and alter her behaviour for herself, or of allowing her the face-saving refuge of being able to pretend that her violence was assumed and that now she chooses to drop it; he also followed the direct and brutal method by which a man tames a hawk. Here a man pits his own will against the bird's, outwatching the bird and denying it food and sleep until it surrenders. If Shakespeare had contented himself with the scenes showing Petruchio putting this method into practice, scenes which also show that he was acting a part and would welcome co-operation, we might agree with Hardin Craig and grant that the hawk-taming motive had lost its crudeness; but Shakespeare expressly thrusts forward a Petruchio glorying in his hawk-taming skill. How, I ask, can we escape from this soliloquy?

> Thus have I politicly begun my reign,
> And 'tis my hope to end successfully.
> My falcon now is sharp and passing empty.
> And till she stoop she must not be full-gorg'd,
> For then she never looks upon her lure.
> Another way I have to man my haggard,
> To make her come, and know her keeper's call,
> That is, to watch her, as we watch these kites

That bate and beat, and will not be obedient.
She eat no meat today, nor none shall eat;
Last night she slept not, nor tonight she shall not; . . .
And thus I'll curb her mad and headstrong humour.
He that knows better how to tame a shrew,
Now let him speak; 'tis charity to show.

(IV, i, 172)

The last couplet is especially baffling, for Petruchio has been using his 'better way' for some time now.

Then there is Petruchio's first entry in I, ii, his meeting with his old friend Hortensio, and the first motion in the process of his courting Katherina Minola. I cannot see this part as suitable to anything but a farce and a crude one at that. Hortensio advances Katherina as 'shrewd and ill-favoured' but very rich; it is only later that he calls her

young and beauteous;
Brought up as best becomes a gentlewoman;

(I, ii, 84)

Whereupon Petruchio protests that money is everything, looks and temper nothing:

Be she as foul as was Florentius' love,
As old as Sibyl, and as curst and shrewd
As Socrates' Xanthippe or a worse—
She moves me not,

(I, ii, 67)

And Grumio, the clown, Petruchio's servant, reinforces the sentiment with

Nay, look you, sir, he tells you flatly what his mind is. Why, give him gold enough and marry him to a puppet or an aglet-baby, or an old trot with ne'er a tooth in her head, though she have as many diseases as two and fifty horses. Why, nothing comes amiss, so money comes withal.

(I, ii, 75)

86

I doubt if it is any use pointing out that in the story of Florentius his ugly bride is rejuvenated and beautified and that this reference contradicts Petruchio's apparent rejection of any concern with his bride's looks, for in this context Florentius' bride is coupled with the Sibyl and exists as a similar comparison might stand in *Charley's Aunt*, when the father decides to take the plunge and aim at the rich old woman for the financial benefit of his son. All the real pointers are here to farce. And had Shakespeare at this stage intended to point to more than farce, he could so easily have shown his Petruchio demanding in his shrew health at least as well as wealth.

I have mentioned the signs of a greater delicacy in Petruchio when he courts Katherina in the first scene of the second act. But the total effect of his courtship is more apt to farce than to comedy. The exchange of wit is hard and heartless, and its coarseness is justified only in a farcical setting. That coarseness is much cruder than anything in the talk between Beatrice and Benedick, and much less called for; since Petruchio meets Katherina for the first time, while Beatrice and Benedick are close friends, having been verbal sparring partners for a long time, hence fit to take liberties with one another.

In sum, when you include all the factors in your ken, you cannot be happy in taking the main plot either as farce or as comedy. It is more comedy than farce but not sufficiently more to enable you to take it serenely as such. All you can do is to admit that the *Taming of the Shrew* suffers from a bad inconsistency and perhaps to conjecture that one of Shakespeare's motives in writing *Much Ado About Nothing* was to mend his failure.

The character of Katherina corresponds fairly closely with the ambiguous quality of the plot in which she figures. I cannot agree with Coghill that her violence is a psychological necessity: 'What choice has Katherina but to show her disdainful temper if she is to keep her self-respect?' Protest can take other forms in civilized society than those extremes of physical violence that provoke the primitive parts of ourselves to easy laughter. Katherina, binding her sister's wrists and beating her, breaking the lute over Hortensio's head, and slapping Petruchio in the face is a figure of farce not of comedy. And yet Shakespeare shows considerable subtlety in the way he develops her character. Katherina wants to be loved and Shakespeare discloses this, not as in the *Taming of a Shrew* by direct self-avowal but by the interest she takes in her sister's suitors:

> Of all thy suitors here I charge thee tell
> Whom thou lov'st best. See thou dissemble not.
> (II, i, 8)

When in the long first scene of act two Petruchio's courtship of Katherina is followed by the formal betrothal before witnesses, she does not follow up her initial protest ('I'll see thee hanged on Sunday first') but acquiesces in silence, showing that in the secrecy of her heart she is not displeased; and when at the time appointed for the wedding Petruchio is not there, for all the hard things she says of him, she sheds tears of honest disappointment. Then, before the final taming, she shows herself wanting to conform to the ordinary ways of society. She joins with the others in imploring Petruchio to stay for the celebrations after the marriage instead of rushing off to his country home. Later she reveals her unacknowledged wish to be a normal girl when the haberdasher brings her the cap, on which she comments thus:

I'll have no bigger; this does fit the time,
And gentlewomen wear such caps as these.

(IV, iii, 69)

A little while ago these would have been reasons for not
liking the cap. She is now half way toward admitting that
she wants Petruchio's love and that she is willing to be
the kind of wife of which convention approves. Of the
ambiguous nature of the culminating scene of surrender I
have already written.

On a balance Katherina exemplifies the central comic
theme of a person erring against the way of the world and
being brought to conform to it, even though part of her
behaviour belongs to a different set of feelings.

iii. THE BIANCA PLOT

I have already pleaded for the excellence of a short passage
in this plot, but more remains to be said in its defence.

It should be obvious that any second plot, even if re-
inforcing or echoing the main plot in certain ways, should
in others be set against it. If not, there will be redundancy,
hence tedium. And yet readers have seemed to demand
the same virtues from both plots of the *Taming of the
Shrew.* They have somehow assumed that the main plot
is more free and natural and that the sub-plot, because cast
in a highly conventional mould, must therefore be inferior.
It would be more reasonable to applaud such a contrast in
the first place and then to go on to ask whether the two
plots are good in their own peculiar ways. It is agreed,
and rightly, that the main plot pleases by its happy im-
petus and by the richness of its diction in certain places. It
is usual to find the sub-plot deficient in these qualities and

hence to condemn it, when it would be fairer to ask whether it contains any different and contrasted virtues. But before I try to answer this question, I must point to another matter, habitually ignored: that the separation between the two plots is far less than assumed, and the common ground much larger. One of the most exuberant parts of the play is that which contains the account of Petruchio's amazing dress for the wedding and of the dreadful old horse on which he has arrived, and later of the bridegroom's outrageous behaviour at the wedding itself. These are usually reckoned parts of the main plot: but with insufficient reason, for it is Biondello who speaks the first account and Gremio the second, and Biondello and Gremio are characters in the second plot. Next, large parts of the main plot are written in that competent, end-stopped, and not especially heightened form of blank verse that forms the staple of Shakespeare's early plays, comedies and histories alike, and which critics used to question as genuine Shakespeare, just because it was no more than work-a-day and not especially exciting. Take this speech of Petruchio, part, as such, of the main plot. He is greeting Vincentio, whom he identifies as father of Lucentio.

> Happily met; the happier for thy son.
> And now by law, as well as reverent age,
> I may entitle thee my loving father:
> The sister to my wife, this gentlewoman,
> Thy son by this hath married. Wonder not,
> Nor be not grieved—she is of good esteem,
> Her dowry wealthy, and of worthy birth;
> Beside, so qualified as may beseem
> The spouse of any noble gentleman.
> Let me embrace with old Vincentio;

And wander we to see thy honest son,
Who will of thy arrival be full joyous.

(IV, v, 58)

There is no difference between this kind of blank verse and the kind that prevails in the sub-plot. The same is true of the doggerel and the prose; they are found equally in both places. With so much in common between the two objects of comparison or contrast, the possible range of discrepancy is much smaller than it is usually assumed to be.

What, then, of those parts of the sub-plot that are plainly peculiar to it? On one of these, the conversation between Lucentio and Biondello on the arrangements for the former's secret marriage I have commented already. Its virtues are brevity, elegance, and delight in a piquant human situation. It does not canvass attention, though it can spring suprises, as in the passage about the wench getting married 'in an afternoon as she went to the garden for parsley to stuff a rabbit' (IV, iv, 97). It is in fact sharply different from the livest things in the main plot, such as Petruchio's stream of abuse of the haberdasher and tailor and their wares:

> O monstrous arrogance! Thou liest, thou thread, thou thimble,
> Thou yard, three-quarters, half-yard, quarter, nail,
> Thou flea, thou nit, thou winter-cricket, thou—
> Brav'd in mine own house with a skein of thread!
> Away, thou rag, thou quantity, thou remnant;
> Or I shall so be mete thee with thy yard
> As thou shalt think on prating whilst thou liv'st!

(IV, iii, 106)

While Biondello's words work neatly and quietly, Petruchio's fairly advertise their propagation. I find the contrast of styles very agreeable.

91

There is a similar lack of ostentation in the frank conventionality of the characters of the sub-plot. Lucentio is the little differentiated lover of classical and Renaissance comedy. Bianca, better differentiated, is of the mainly passive type. Biondello is the stock cheeky page, whatever his virtues in the part. Tranio derives from the clever slave of Roman comedy who is active in promoting the action. Gremio is the elderly rich lover, destined to be thwarted or at least scored off by his juniors. It must be owing to this seeming conventionality that critics have not given these characters much of a chance. There is little life in the nominal hero (or victim) of the Bianca plot; and it is Tranio who propels the action and who of all the characters best corresponds with Petruchio in the Katherina plot. Though the son of a sail-maker of Bergamo, he has observed acutely the manners of his betters and has picked up enough tags of Italian to carry conviction in polite society. In his first speech he can talk of Aristotle and Ovid, knowing at least what kind of writers they are and can play on words in the approved style:

> Let's be no Stoics nor no stocks, I pray.
>
> (I, i, 31)

He appears first as Lucentio's confidential servant; and Lucentio depends on him sufficiently to ask his advice. It is when he personates his master that he comes into his own. He dominates the other suitors of Bianca from the beginning. Meeting them and Petruchio, he asks in brisk rhymed doggerel the way to Baptista's house; and Biondello helps him out with, 'He that has the two fair daughters; is't he you mean?' (I, ii, 218) And the dialogue goes on:

Tra. Even he, Biondello,
Gre. Hark you, sir; you mean not her too?[1]

(I, ii, 220)*

Tranio is not put out by Gremio's threatening tone and answers:

Tra. Perhaps him and her, sir; what have you to do?
Pet. Not her that chides, sir, at any hand, I pray.
Tra. I love no chiders, sir. Biondello, let's away.
Luc. (in the background). Well begun, Tranio.
Hor. Sir, a word ere you go.
Are you a suitor to the maid you talk of, yea or no?
Tra. And if I be, sir, is it any offence?
Gre. No; if without more words you will get you hence.
Tra. Why, sir, I pray, are not the streets as free
For me as for you?
Gre. But so is not she.
Tra. For what reason, I beseech you?
Gre. For this reason, if you'll know,
That she's the choice love of Signior Gremio.
Hor. That she's the chosen of Signior Hortensio.

(I, ii, 222)*

Whereupon, Tranio, disdainful of a quarrel in the street, assumes a lordly air and proceeds to reason with the two suitors in cool blank verse:

Tra. Softly, my masters! If you be gentlemen,
Do me this right—hear me with patience.
Baptista is a noble gentleman,
To whom my father is not all unknown,

(I, ii, 234)

Note the patronizing toning down of the last line. Tranio with 'not all unknown' assumes that Baptista is on more

[1] Should be read: 'Hárk you, sír; you mèan not her tóo?'

93

familiar terms with *his* father than he is with Gremio and Hortensio or any of their belongings. He goes on:

> *Tra.* And, were his daughter fairer than she is,
> She may more suitors have, and me for one.[1]
> Fair Leda's daughter had a thousand wooers;
> Then well one more may fair Bianca have;
>
> (I, ii, 238)

The suitors cannot resist Tranio's lordly reasonableness, though Gremio grumbles; and Petruchio explains to Tranio the present ban on all Bianca's wooers and the consequent truce between them. Whereupon, Tranio gets in an invitation to drink together:

> *Tra.* Please ye we may contrive[2] this afternoon,
> And quaff carouses to our mistress' health;
> And do as adversaries do in law—
> Strive mightily, but eat and drink as friends.
>
> (I, ii, 272)

Tranio holds the initiative throughout the scene and dominates it. His impersonation of the grandee convinces entirely. His next ordeal is to outbid Gremio when Baptista decides to auction Bianca. He takes big risks, being extremely familiar with Baptista and trumping Gremio's offers with gross and glaring exaggeration. Baptista, the betrothal of Katherina concluded, remarks on the desperate pact he has made. Whereupon, Tranio, referring to Katherina, says to him, ' 'Twas a commodity lay

---

[1] I do not see the logic of this couplet, though it does not seem to have troubled the editors. Surely logic demands 'less fair' instead of 'fairer'. Then the argument would be: even if Bianca were less fair, she would deserve more than two suitors. Helen had 1000; so a girl very much less fair would deserve, say, at least a dozen.

[2] *Contrive, wear* or *while away.* Doubtless, Tranio uses this rare word, found in Spenser, to show his own rare quality.

fretting by you' (II, i, 220), with *fretting* meaning both 'going rotten' and 'behaving peevishly'. He is beginning to gain confidence and follow what may be a natural bent to bluff self-assertion. In the bargaining that follows he bears down Gremio with no pretence of finesse. To Gremio's triumphant advancement of an argosy ('What, have I choked you with an argosy?'), he retorts:

> Gremio, 'tis known my father hath no less
> Than three great argosies, besides two galliasses,
> And twelve tight galleys. These will I assure her,
>
> (II, i, 369)

And then he mutters to himself:

> And twice as much whate'er thou off'rest next.

Tranio knows his men. Baptista is not offended by his familiarity, and Gremio never suspects that he is bluffing. He accepts Tranio's account of his father's wealth and merely asks how much of it his son can be sure of, when it comes to the point:

> Sirrah young gamester, your father were a fool
> To give thee all, and in his waning age
> Set foot under thy table. Tut, a toy!
> An old Italian fox is not so kind, my boy.
>
> (II, i, 392)

He goes out, and Tranio's comment on him is:

> A vengeance on your crafty withered hide!
> Yet I have fac'd it with a card of ten.
> 'Tis in my head to do my master good:
> I see no reason but suppos'd Lucentio
> Must get a father, call'd suppos'd Vincentio.
>
> (II, i, 396)

Once again Tranio dominates his scene, which, incidentally, is extremely lively and well fitted to the stage.

Later, during the scene of Petruchio's wedding, Lucentio and Tranio find a few minutes to discuss their affairs; and it is Tranio who is best alive to the need of finding a bogus father to confirm that Lucentio will indeed

> make assurance here in Padua
> Of greater sums than I have promised.
>
> (III, ii, 130)

And when Biondello reports the approach of a likely looking man for the purpose, Tranio is quick to invent a reason why natives of Mantua, where the new arrival lives, had better conceal their presence in Padua; fashioning the man thus to agree to impersonate Lucentio's father. When the Pedant has posed as Vincentio and satisfied Baptista and articles for the marriage are to be drawn up, Tranio achieves the height of courtesy in the way he offers his lodging for the meeting-place with the scrivener, apologizing for the 'thin and slender pittance' (IV, iv, 61) which is all he can offer as entertainment at so short notice. Even when the true Vincentio turns up and Tranio knows his game is lost, he does not surrender without a struggle but accuses him of being mad in claiming to be Lucentio's father and calls for an officer to take him to gaol. No wonder Vincentio meditates special vengeance on him.

In the last scene, when Lucentio assumes his proper identity and welcomes all the company for dessert after the great feast to celebrate the three marriages, Tranio is not forgotten but has his past action referred to and is allowed to initiate another. Petruchio, cheated of his 'bitter jest or two' (V, ii, 45) with Bianca through her withdrawal, followed by that of the other two brides, brings Tranio into the picture by addressing him and calling for 'a health to all that shot and miss'd'. He is here thinking first of Tranio and all he did to 'shoot' Bianca and of the way Tranio's actions, through the arrival of Vincentio, foundered in the end in favour of the alternative method of the clandestine wedding. Tranio reminds Petruchio that he was not hunting Bianca for himself:

> O, sir, Lucentio slipp'd me like his greyhound,
> Which runs himself, and catches for his master.
>
> (V, ii, 52)

And the dialogue proceeds:

> *Petr.* A good swift simile, but something currish.
> *Tra.* 'Tis well, sir, that you hunted for yourself;
> 'Tis thought your deer does hold you at a bay.
>
> (V, ii, 55)

And it is this reference to Katherina that propels the action of the wager. It is as if, in this unexpected place, Shakespeare must needs emphasize Tranio's gift for initiative and his correspondence with Petruchio in his own part of the action.

Tranio, then, is a major[1] character and he offers splendid scope to an actor. He helps powerfully to give weight to the sub-plot of the *Taming of the Shrew*.

I must add a word on Biondello. He is consistent and makes an excellent acting part. He first enters just as his master and Tranio have changed clothes; and his answer to Lucentio's 'Sirrah, where have you been?' is

> Where have I been! Nay, how now! where are you?
> Master, has my fellow Tranio stol'n your clothes?
> Or you stol'n his? or both? Pray, what's the news?
>
> (I, i, 217)

---

[1] In the sense of having a big part to play, not of being one of the 'great' characters in Shakespeare like Shylock or Malvolio.

SHAKESPEARE'S EARLY COMEDIES

And this accent of gaiety fails in none of his speeches.
Take the one in which he announces the arrival of a man
who may personate Vincentio:

> *Bion.* O master, master, I have watch'd so long
> That I am dog-weary; but at last I spied
> An ancient angel coming down the hill
> Will serve the turn.
> *Tra.*   What is he, Biondello?
> *Bion.* Master, a mercatante or a pedant,
> I know not what; but formal in apparel,
> In gait and countenance surely like a father.
>   (IV, ii, 59)

And when Tranio tells the Pedant that he rather resembles
his father Biondello comments, 'As much as an apple doth
an oyster' (IV, iii, 101).

Gremio is a stock character of traditional comedy but a
satisfactory example of the stock: stupid, gullible, and ridiculous in seeking to marry a young girl; and individual-
ized by a grudging, acidulous way of speaking.

Baptista is on the same level: the respectable wealthy
citizen, the worried father, the seeker for a quiet life.
Again, a satisfactory but not conspicuous character. I cannot see him as exceptionally mercenary and someone to be
escaped from, as Coghill does. Rather he is a conventional
comic character, taking a necessary part in the game but
not giving to that game any animating colour.

Bianca is something more. Again, I cannot join Coghill
in villainizing her. She is of little weight but she is a clear
and convincing picture of a pretty, sly little thing. Looking back on her first and only speech in the first scene in
which she appears, we see that she affects the good girl
with a completeness that cannot be sincere. Her father has
ordered her into the house, which implies not just tem-

porary withdrawal but an indefinite immurement; and she comments:

> Sister, content you in my discontent.
> Sir, to your pleasure humbly I subscribe;
> My books and instruments shall be my company,
> On them to look, and practise by myself.
>
> (I, i, 80)

We see that the first line is neatly-calculated coals of fire, and the humble sentiments of the rest are aimed at impressing the listening suitors. Her true nature comes out in the first scene of act three, when Lucentio and Hortensio in disguise come to instruct her in literature and music. As they wrangle about priority, she is cool (and we may infer, delighted) in assuming command.

> Why, gentlemen, you do me double wrong
> To strive for that which resteth in my choice . . .
> And to cut off all strife: here sit we down;
> Take you your instrument, play you the whiles!
> His lecture will be done ere you have tun'd.
>
> (II, i, 16)

And she is equally cool in entering on her intrigue with Lucentio. The strokes may be slight but they characterize Bianca quickly enough. And they prepare us sufficiently for her answer in the last scene of all when the husbands send for their wives. Unlike Hortensio's widow, she does not pronounce defiance by telling her husband to come to her but feigns that she is busy and cannot come. She is still the sly one. More significantly, she continues to confuse appearance and reality, or at least to attempt to do so, for by now we know that her initial meekness was appearance only.

In talking of the characters of the Bianca plot, I have

99

mentioned scenes in which they occur. I have also pointed to the excellence of the little scene where Biondello tells Lucentio of the arrangements for the clandestine wedding. To persuade the reader further (for he is probably prejudiced pretty deeply against the Bianca plot and will need a good deal of persuading) that this plot contains good comic episodes, I ask him to consider a scene I have just referred to: Bianca's lesson in literature and music. In itself it is the stock stuff of the domestic comedy of intrigue, and what originality and distinction it has will depend entircly on the treatment. It shows Bianca waiting to be taught, while Lucentio disguised as a schoolmaster and Hortensio as a musicmaster, quarrel, as rivals in love of course have to do, about who shall get in his lesson first. The scene opens when they have been quarrelling for some time; and the ostensible occasion of their quarrel is the relative merit of literature and music. The situation plays up perfectly to the overriding theme of appearance and reality, for the real cause of the quarrel is not artistic at all but personal. The Folio stage direction is simply 'Enter Lucentio, Hortensio, and Bianca' and I cannot accept the elaborate one constructed by the *New Cambridge Shakespeare* editors, 'Bianca and Hortensio, disguised as Licio, are seated with a lute; Lucentio, disguised as Cambio, standing a little apart, waiting his turn. Hortensio takes Bianca's hand in his to teach her fingering.' On the contrary, the first fifteen lines make it clear that the lesson has not yet begun and that the two men enter arguing about the relative status of their different arts on the assumption that the man who professes the superior art will have first turn. When they have all entered Bianca's room, Hortensio makes a dash 'forward, and Lucentio stops him with

Fiddler, forbear; you grow too forward, sir.
Have you so soon forgot the entertainment
Her sister Katherine welcom'd you withal?

(III, i, 1)

Hortensio's answer does little, as it stands, to follow up
this excellent provocative beginning, because the first line
is defective and has been either given up as hopeless or
completed in a way that heads one off the point of the
dialogue. This is the whole speech:

But, wrangling pedant, this is
The patroness of heavenly harmony.
Then give me leave to have prerogative;
And when in music we have spent an hour,
Your lecture shall have leisure for as much.

(III, i, 4)

Most editors despair of the first line and quote Theobald's
completion:

She is a shrew; but, wrangling pedant, this is
The patroness of heavenly harmony.

Theobald assumed that 'this' was Bianca and proceeded to
build on this assumption and add a reference to Katherina
in contrast. But 'this' is clearly not Bianca. The two men
are agreed that Katherina is a shrew and that Bianca is
perfection: they have nothing here to quarrel about. The
quarrel is about the merits of music and poetry; and 'this'
must refer to something pertinent to that quarrel. Surely
the obvious procedure is to ask who is the 'patroness of
heavenly harmony'; and the obvious answer is one of the
Muses and, if one of the Muses, Urania. Urania was the
Muse of the heavens and their mathematics; and we must
remember that Petruchio presented Hortensio to Baptista as 'Cunning in music and the mathematics' (II, i, 56).

But according to the Pythagorean interpretation of the Muses Urania was also the Muse in charge of the music of the heaven of the fixed stars, as Polymnia was in charge of the Music of the sphere in which Saturn was set, and so on. Shakespeare knew the Pythagorean doctrine, which was one of the age's commonplaces, found for instance in so public a book as Conti's *Mythologia*. He was even to improve on it shortly after in the fifth act of the *Merchant of Venice* when he made Lorenzo say

> There's not the smallest orb which thou behold'st
> But in his motion like an angel sings,
> (*Merchant of Venice*, V, i, 60)

Urania, the ruling spirit of all these singing stars in the fixed sphere of heaven, is, in Shakespeare's mythology, most emphatically the patroness of heavenly harmony. Read, therefore,

> But, wrangling pedant, this Urania is
> The patroness of heavenly harmony,

and you get an obvious sense. In the quarrel before entry Hortensio had already mentioned Urania, and 'this' refers back to the previous mention. Armed by the cosmic commonplace, Hortensio then goes on to reassert his claim to give the first lesson. Lucentio continues the argument and parries Hortensio's claim that he, as representative of the Muse of the fixed stars, should have precedence by another commonplace: that the function of music is recreation after tougher studies:

> Preposterous ass, that never read so far
> To know the cause why music was ordain'd!
> Was it not to refresh the mind of man
> After his studies or his usual pain?

Then give me leave to read philosophy,
And while I pause serve in your harmony.

(III, i, 9)

Note '*your* harmony': confirming that the patroness of
heavenly harmony cannot be Bianca. Whereupon Hortensio's temper rises and he exclaims: 'Sirrah, I will not bear
these braves of thine.' Violence now threatens; and it is
time for Bianca to intervene. So she puts the two wranglers
in their place by telling them that she is no longer a
schoolchild and that the decision as to precedence is hers.
They will all sit down, and Lucentio will begin his lesson
while Hortensio tunes his instrument.

To tell us all this Shakespeare takes only twenty-five
lines; and in them he has created the cleanest and most
delightful comic situation. The picture of the two quarrelling men, each intent on his amorous pursuit, indifferent
to the art he is supposed to be professing and yet advancing the correct commonplaces in the defence of it, is
classically comic. The two are so utterly off their guard,
so vulnerable if watched. And watched they are, first by
the coolly rejoicing Bianca and then by ourselves, who see
what fools the passion of love has made of these men and
what a cat Bianca is in enjoying the quarrel. Shakespeare
puts us into the perfect comic state of mind: superior and
detached, because at the moment we are not tempted to
comparable folly and malice; and yet social and sympa-
thetic because we know that this is the way you or I might
behave in comparable circumstances.

For the rest of the scene Bianca takes control, with the
quarrel still spluttering in the background, and succeeds
neatly enough in putting the two lovers where she wants
them. And the action is further advanced by Hortensio's
beginning to cool off as he sees the way things are going.

The comedy is light, but I cannot see how it could be bettered.

iv. APPEARANCE AND REALITY

The overriding theme, the theme that unites the play's two plots, is that of appearance and reality. The girl who appeared the shrew turns out the obedient wife; and the girl who appeared meek turns out on marriage not to be so. It is the theme of Crabbe's tale, *The Wager*, where the wife who is dictatorial in small matters shows sympathy with her husband in large; and the wife who professes to yield on every point, when there is a real clash of wills, gets her own way by feigned faintings and sickness. However, it does not get you far to proclaim the appearance-reality theme; for what matters so much more than the theme itself is the way it is executed.[1] Does it genuinely pervade the whole? or is it something recognized by the intellect and coolly and consciously pursued?

I fear the answer must be ambiguous. And the ambiguity follows the lines of division that appeared when the question of farce or comedy in the main plot was my topic. In those parts where crude farce lingers the theme of appearance and reality not only fails to pervade but simply is absent. Katherina is not a girl who grows up and reveals hidden things in her character but remains the same girl, only with her will broken. Petruchio, confident in the doctrine that wives must submit to their husbands and in his ability to enforce it, is equally unchanging. But in those parts where Katherina is a psychological case, her natural

[1] See M. Lüthi's extended treatment of the theme in *Shakespeare's Dramen* (Berlin, 1957). See also the Appendix, p. 209, on 'The Fairytale Element in *The Taming of the Shrew*'.

affections and good intellect thwarted, to be cured by a seemingly insensitive but actually shrewd and understanding man, the theme is pervasive. It is equally pervasive in the Induction, but with a difference. The pervasiveness is too obvious to need much comment; but it may be worth remarking that it arises naturally in the thirty-third line when the Lord, seeing Sly on the ground motionless, asks whether he is dead or drunk; that is really or apparently dead. He learns that, though he would from his surroundings appear cold, Sly is in fact warmed with drink. He then says Sly looks like a swine, implying the discrepancy between swinish appearance and human, immortal, interior; and this thought leads on to the conjecture whether it would not be possible to manipulate appearance and reality in another direction and make the human being, now swinelike, resemble a man of the highest rank; with who knows what results? The experiment is elaborated, and evidence accumulated that Sly's past life has been fiction and his present situation the reality. He is furnished with all the appearances of rank, including that of a dutiful wife, who says to him:

> My husband and my lord, my lord and husband;
> I am your wife in all obedience.
>
> (Induction, ii, 104)

Actually it is a boy, dressed as a woman, who speaks; and this double impersonation both in itself constitutes a fitting climax and pausing point in the present action and serves to introduce the theme of the inset play: that of apparent and real dutifulness in wives.

Thus the Induction, which most readers agree excels all other parts of the play in sustained charm, both succeeds in exploiting the overriding theme and in leading up to the play that follows it. But it does more: it makes us reflect, as nothing else in the whole play does, not only on the facts of appearance and reality in the business of social life but on the abstract question of what is appearance and what reality. Louis Cazamian, asking what the Induction means, wrote:

> Une mise en scène imaginée par le caprice d'un grand seigneur, ou le symbole frappant de la relativité qui contredit à tout moment notre foi naïve aux valeurs absolues? Il est risible de voir la balourdise réelle de Sly s'affirmer pesamment dans le monde illusoire où il s'est éveillé. Mais si cette illusion se prolongeait, où serait en fin de compte la realité, où le songe?[1]

And he compares Sancho Panza in a similar mystification. Cazamian is right. There is exquisite comedy in Sly, newly awakened in his gorgeous surroundings, demanding a pot of the smallest ale; and there is the hint, through his bewilderment and his final acquiescence in the reality of the moment, that the limits of the apparent and the real are not easily charted. Such thoughts would well occur in an age of allegory, with Spenser the chief poet, to any thoughtful man; but to a Shakespeare, with his unparalleled gift for observing people, they might also have occurred through the impact of certain types of character and of experience. We have all encountered men who on most of the evidence are nothing but façade but who manipulate that façade with a skill or genius which, as it were, makes it grow backward and provide, if not reality, something so like it as to serve as well. And there is the spectacle of men accepting beliefs on a basis of apparently shallow expediency or despair and finding in process of time that these have spread or eaten into the substance of their natures. It would indeed be possible to tell the story of the

[1] *L'humour de Shakespeare* (Paris, 1945), p. 59.

emperor's clothes another way, cutting out the child, prolonging the perambulation of the city, and causing the emperor to find that when he reached the palace he was indeed wearing a thin nylon dressing-gown.

In the sub-plot the theme of appearance and reality is treated superficially, on the whole. Bianca, of course, accords with the main plot, but Lucentio in no way matches Petruchio. He exemplifies the theme in no more profound way than pretending to be his own servant. It is possible that Shakespeare meant something more through Tranio: namely that, though in condition the son of a sail-maker of Bergamo and a servant, in true quality he was a better man than his master and by nature a nobleman. But generally the theme is exemplified, as it is through Lucentio, by people pretending to be other than they are either by false assumptions about themselves or by impersonation. Here Shakespeare followed one of his models, Ariosto's *I Suppositi* in Gascoigne's translation *The Supposes*, in the introduction to which Gascoigne defines a 'suppose' as 'a mistaking or imagination of one thing for another'. The various disguises or Gremio's picture of himself as young enough to court a teenager exploit but superficially the theme of appearance and reality. In a minor way they may contribute to the moral I have already applied to the play on its social side: that in the traffic of men and women you had better look below the surface.

Thus, the theme of appearance and reality, though clearly paramount, is not presented with sufficient steadiness of significance to be allowed any very substantial weight. The unity it offers may give superficial pleasure and assure us that Shakespeare took a certain amount of trouble: but we must beware of dwelling too seriously upon it.

V. ROMANCE

There is less of the element of romance and the feelings this arouses in the *Taming of the Shrew* than in any of Shakespeare's comedies.[1] Peter Alexander[2] may well be right in saying that the main plot might be

> a version of one of the great themes of literature, a comic treatment of the perilous maiden theme, where the lady is death to any suitor who woos her except the hero, in whose hands her apparent vices turn to virtues;

but it is a version robbed of any sense of the ordeal or of the good day's work accomplished. Again, if you are anthropologically inclined, you could make the play a study in exogamy in which the two sturdy aliens, Petruchio and Lucentio, invade and capture the two sisters whom the local boys either fight shy of as beyond their control or are forced to abandon. But I do not see any but extremists doing that. Consider the last scene. Here, if anywhere, we are likely to find the romantic strain. Instead we find pure, or almost pure, comedy. I say 'almost pure', because in Petruchio's

> Katherine, that cap of yours becomes you not:
> Off with that bauble, throw it underfoot.
> (V, ii, 121)

I cannot, personally, fail to hear the crack of the tamer's whip and to feel the momentary return to crude farce. Otherwise, the scene, founded though it is on a primitive

[1] (Editor's note.) Author's memorandum here reads: 'Section on romance must be re-written in view of Lüthi's comparison (op. cit. pp. 210–11) with story of King Thrushbeard.' See Appendix.

[2] *Shakespeare's Life and Art* (London, 1939), p. 71.

fable, has to do with social life in a civilized society. And it ends not on any note of imagined bliss and living happily ever after but with a sophisticated leaving of things open: with the demonstration that in our common life you must be ready for anything; *you never can tell.*

vi. COMEDY

Though the last scene lacks romance it contains in a highly representative manner those things in the play which I believe best characterize it and give us the greatest pleasure. It shows us all the main characters, after the triple marriage and the wedding feast at Baptista's, assembled at Lucentio's lodging for dessert. Even disappointed Gremio is there; and Tranio after his duties (Folio stage-direction: *The Servingmen with Tranio bringing in a Banquet*) stays and takes part in the talk on very equal terms, with Biondello there too to carry messages. All is easy and intimate; and the talk, though its kind of wit is not ours, convinces us that real people are talking. Shakespeare in fact exercises here his adorable gift of making us feel close to his characters, almost of allowing his readers to share in the social life he presents so lucidly. I have called this last scene 'representative', and so it is, but not entirely; for the Induction, though equally successful in making us feel close to the persons, extends the social range both downward and upward: down to Sly and the company he consorts with and refers to and up to the noblemen with their huntsmen and the itinerant players to whose employment the merchant wealth of Padua or the squire-status of Petruchio in his country house would not extend. All through the play there is the impression of the genuine domestic life, humanizing the cruder parts of the main plot and bringing to life the rigid and potentially arid conventions on which the subplot is founded.

The most sustained picture of domestic life is that of Petruchio's country house. True, the things that happened there were exceptional but at the same time we gather the sense of what was normal. Grumio in one sense is the conventional, necessary clown but he is also that genuinely recurrent character, the humorist of the gang. Arriving after the dreadful journey he calls Curtis, one of the servants, who enters and asks who 'calls so coldly'. Grumio, undefeated, answers, 'A piece of ice. If thou doubt it, thou mayst slide from my shoulder to my heel with no greater a run but my head and my neck' (IV, i, 12), and we feel that this is the kind of thing the other servants expect of him. And when, having made sure that the supper is ready, the house trimmed, rushes strewed, cobwebs swept, the servingmen in their new fustian and so on, he comes to the story of the journey from Padua, he has enough spirit left to parody the narrative art by recounting all the things that he would have told, 'hadst thou not crossed me', and the romances themselves by ending with

> how I lost my crupper—with many things of worthy memory, which now shall die in oblivion, and thou return unexperienc'd to thy grave.
>
> (IV, i, 70)

And later the visits from the tradesmen complete the picture of life in the country.

In this and the other renderings of the domestic life lies our best chance of finding the common factor in a play full of delightful things but conspicuous more for richness than for homogeneity.

NOTE

I have mentioned the *Taming of a Shrew* in my text but without saying what I think its relationship is to Shakespeare's play. I find so vast a discrepancy between the excellent plotting and the violently fluctuating execution of *A Shrew* that I cannot think it a play in its own right and Shakespeare's original. It is a garbled version of something else; and I incline to disagree with Alexander that it derives from *The Shrew* and to agree with Ten Brink, Hardin Craig (*George F. Reynolds Festschrift*, Boulder, 1945), and G. I. Duthie (*Review of English Studies*, 1943, pp. 337–56) that both *Shrews* have a common original. Further, I think the plotting of both plays to be too good for their original to be by any other hand than Shakespeare's.

Chapter V

THE TWO GENTLEMEN OF
VERONA

i. THE CENTRAL FLAW

THIS is one of the least loved of Shakespeare's plays; and some of its critics have made one feel that the chief fault lies with the ending. Having rescued Silvia from outlaws in the forest on the confines of Milanese and Mantuan territory, Proteus crowns a series of villainies and meannesses by offering to rape her in presence of Julia, who, ever faithful, has followed him in male disguise and has been accepted as his page. Valentine, who has been watching him in concealment, steps out and prevents the outrage. He then spends eleven lines in denouncing his former friend. Proteus replies with four and a half lines professing utter repentance and a state of mind as true in its present anguish as its past sins were great. Finally, Valentine gives six and a half lines to accepting Proteus's repentance and surrendering his Silvia to him to demonstrate the perfection of his friendship. It has been pretty well agreed that this scene is morally and dramatically monstrous: that a proposal to hand over a girl to the man who has just proposed to rape her revolts our moral sense and that the perfunctory speed with which these staggering events are recounted can only provoke our laughter.

If critics have generally agreed in condemning the episode, they have differed in the ways they have acted on their condemnation. The *New Cambridge Shakespeare*

editors have sought to relieve Shakespeare of the blame
by attributing the present state of the text to an abbrevia-
tor. The original would have been very much longer and
not open to the same blame. Vyvyan[1] would mitigate
Shakespeare's crime by making the whole play more of
an allegory than it has ever been thought, thus minimi-
zing any allegiance the scene might owe to the standards
of normal life. It might also be possible to make out a
case for the scene's burlesquing the traditional doctrine
of friendship's claims being paramount and to cite the
analogy of Peele's *Old Wives' Tale*. Here, in just the same
place in the play, is a clear burlesque of the doctrine.
Jack's ghost and Eumenides are sworn friends and must
go shares in everything. Jack's ghost claims his share in
Eumenides's Delia and orders him to bisect her, which
Eumenides makes preparations to do.

I doubt all these mitigations as much as I doubt the
one attempt of which I am aware to justify the episode
as it stands, that of W. W. Lawrence in his *Shakespeare's
Problem Comedies*.[2] Lawrence thinks that the convention
of the paramount exactions of friendship was so strong
that an Elizabethan audience would have accepted without difficulty both the morality and the abruptness of the
scene in question. He cites the story of Titus and Gisippus
and goes on:

> The *Two Gentlemen* has been . . . taken to be mainly a love-
> story, whereas it is really a tale glorifying friendship. Even after
> the traitorous Proteus betrays him at the end, in a scene which
> generations of critics have misunderstood, Valentine is still the
> perfect friend, ready, when Proteus professes repentance, to sacri-
> fice his lady without consulting her, in order to prove the depth
> of his devotion to Proteus and the sincerity of his forgiveness.

[1] Op. cit., pp. 130–135.   [2] New York, 1931, p. 24.

Much as I admire Lawrence's book, here I am in perfect disagreement with him, holding that Shakespeare's intention to glorify friendship is both unsuccessful and secondary. Take first his reference to the old story of Titus and Gisippus. Lawrence thinks it serves to support Shakespeare's treatment of the theme of friendship; on the contrary I think it most important as showing it up. The story, based on earlier material, is told as the eighth story of the tenth day of Boccaccio's *Decameron*. Elyot in the twelfth chapter of the second book of the *Governour* gave his own version of it, 'whereby is fully declared the figure of perfect amity'. What is common to the *Two Gentlemen* and the story of Titus and Gisippus is that two friends fall in love with the same girl and that the girl's original lover, to whom she is plighted, surrenders her to his friend when he learns that this friend is also in love. But there are radical differences. In the story Titus suffers fierce remorse for his passion and is so torn by the competing stresses of love and duty that he takes to his bed and is near death; after which Gisippus visits him and only by pressure extracts his secret from him. In the play Proteus hardly listens to conscience, maintains excellent health while deceiving his friend and others, while Valentine remains ignorant of Proteus's love till he witnesses him intending a rape of the object of it. In the *Governour* especially, Titus's plight is vividly and movingly presented. When he knew himself to be far-gone in love

the miserable Titus, withdrawing him as it were to his study, all tormented and oppressed with love, threw himself on a bed and there rebuking his own most dispiteful unkindness, which, by the sudden sight of a maiden, he had conspired again his most dear friend Gisippus, against all humanity and reason, he cursed his fate or constellation and wished that he had never come to Athens.

Gisippus protests that he must know the trouble and that he will go to all lengths to alleviate it.

With which words, obtestations, and tears of Gisippus, Titus constrained, all blushing and ashamed, holding down his head, brought forth with great difficulty his words in this wise. 'My dear and most loving friend, withdraw your friendly offers, cease of your courtesy, refrain your tears and regretting, take rather your knife and slay me here where I lie, or otherwise take vengeance on me, most miserable and false traitor unto you, and of all other most worthy to suffer most shameful death.'[1]

Proteus's soliloquy after falling in love with Silvia (II, vi) is mainly a coolly stated series of quibbles in justification of his treachery. The nearest he gets to remorse is his

Fie, fie, unreverend tongue, to call her bad
Whose sovereignty so oft thou hast preferr'd
With twenty thousand soul-confirming oaths!
(II, vi, 13)

And he goes on to quench any flicker of remorse with

I will forget that Julia is alive,
Rememb'ring that my love to her is dead;
And Valentine I'll hold an enemy,
Aiming at Silvia as a sweeter friend.
I cannot now prove constant to myself
Without some treachery us'd to Valentine.
(II, vi, 27)

Another difference between novel and play is that Gisippus's surrender of his lady is reasonable as well as idealistic, for he recognizes that though he is truly in love with her he is so less madly and dangerously than Titus. It is reasonable that the man with the greater need should get his desire. Valentine's surrender of Silvia to a man who has behaved outrageously and whose professed repentance has not begun to be tested offends utterly against reason. But such unreasonableness and with it all the offence of the 'infamous finale' pale before Shakespeare's major dramatic crimes committed much earlier on, of failing to make credible Proteus's treachery and of missing the moral conflict, so well presented by Boccaccio and Elyot, that alone can give the situation its greatest interest. Up to the time of his treachery Proteus is made to appear the highest type of man.[1] Lucetta, Julia's quick-witted waiting-woman, thinks him the best of the many good suitors of her mistress. Valentine, recom-

---

[1] Lüthi (op. cit., p. 192) argues interestingly in a contrary sense, Proteus's name indicates inconstancy, and his words in the first scene, 'Thou, Julia, thou hast metamorphosed me,' etc., corroborate this indication. He shows a lack of will power in yielding without a struggle to his father's commands to leave Verona and Julia. His father showed his fickle temperament in changing his whim at the suggestion of a servant; and we may expect a son to inherit a father's temperament. We have therefore been prepared for Proteus's sudden change from honourable to dishonourable behaviour. I should retort that the love-signs Proteus enumerates in his soliloquy in I, i are conventional and could apply to any lover, faithful or unfaithful. The word 'metamorphosed' points neither way, for Speed says of the new love of Valentine, who was faithful, 'Now you are metamorphosed with a mistress' (II, i). For a young man to obey a peremptory father need not indicate instability; and the text suggests that Proteus had simply no option. To introduce a father's resolve to send his son abroad through the report of a brother's opinion (an opinion that confirms his existing one) is no more than a device to enliven an episode and tells us nothing about that father's character. I grant that the name *Proteus* might mean something, but scarcely if uncorroborated. And I hold that, in a reading that does not look, in preconception, for a single line of evidence, the *Two Gentlemen* gives no indication beforehand that Proteus was to behave treacherously and meanly.

mending Proteus to the Duke of Milan, says of him that he knows him as himself, 'for from our infancy/ We have convers'd and spent our hours together' (II, iv, 58). And he sums up his praises with

> He is complete in feature and in mind,
> With all good grace to grace a gentleman.
>
> (II, iv, 69)

After such statements Proteus's treachery comes as a wanton surprise. As to the moral conflicts, it is astonishing that Shakespeare with the example of Elyot in front of him and destined a few years later to turn the conflicts in the mind of Brutus over the fate of his friend to the highest dramatic account should here have failed so signally in dramatic intelligence. I doubt if such a failure can be matched in the rest of Shakespeare. Anyhow, it prevents the many beauties in the play having any great cumulative effect and it puts into the shade the faults at the end from which this discussion began.

There is another, and different, consequence of Shakespeare's lapse in treating the theme of friendship: the improbability that he began his play with that theme the master theme, as Lawrence maintains he did. Had he thus begun, I cannot see how he could have flouted its dramatic potentialities. But, if he used it as a mere supporting or contrasted theme, it is possible to conjecture with some show of plausibility why he acted as he did. To arrive at such a conjecture I shall need to turn to the other theme of the play, that of love.

ii. THE LOVE THEME

For the theme of the two friends' having their friendship tested through loving the same girl Shakespeare had plenty of parallels but he did not use any of them as a direct original. It is otherwise with the greater part of the love theme, which was derived from an episode in Montemayor's *Diana Enamorada*. These facts make it more likely than not that Shakespeare took off from Montemayor and then adapted the theme of friendship to what he considered the needs of the theme of love. This likelihood is enhanced by the closeness with which he followed his original. Montemayor's story of Felix and Felismena is triangular and concerns the love of one man for two women, with the title characters corresponding to Proteus and Julia, and Celia corresponding to Silvia. There is no Valentine in Montemayor. But Felix has a page, Fabius, before he engages Felismena, disguised as a boy, for a second. Thus Fabius in function, though not at all in character, corresponds to Launce. Some of Shakespeare's scenes follow Montemayor's closely. Felismena has a waiting-maid, Rosina, who suggested Lucetta. Like Felismena, Julia first rejects and then recovers her lover's letter. Both Felix and Proteus are sent away from home by suspicious fathers. Felismena and Julia follow their lovers in boy's dress and are taken by their hosts to witness their lovers serenading other women. They both become pages to their lovers. Celia and Silvia know that the men who court them have deserted their old loves and repel their advances. Felismena and Julia are both employed to promote their masters' courtships and both find favour with the women they visit for the purpose. But they differ in the way they carry out this duty. Julia, though the gentler character, does not intend to do her harrowing duty too successfully. But Felismena, a more passionate and complicated character, courts Celia fiercely for her lover, partly to give herself the pleasure of the utmost pain and partly to prevent her lover's flight, which she fears might ensue if Celia continues to reject him too harshly. Her fierce courtship causes Celia first to answer Felix more kindly than she feels, then to fall in love with the disguised Felismena, and finally to die of that love. In spite of these differences Shakespeare followed not only most of Montemayor's incidents but the general disposition that animated them.

The pastoral romance, like other civilized narrative of the Renaissance, aimed at entertainment through recounting a series of events surprising in themselves but usually conventional through frequent previous use. It exacted a high standard of elegance in shaping and diction, in contrast to the chaos of marvels found in the more popular and primitive romances like *Huon of Bordeaux*. It used a conventional psychology and did not insist on arousing the genuine depths of human feeling. Nevertheless the option remained of doing so from time to time, as occasion offered.

In the *Two Gentlemen* Shakespeare took off from Renaissance romance and from Montemayor in particular. This was a new venture, and to meet it he invented a new kind of verse. Geoffrey Bullough[1] was right in calling the play one of technical experiment and also one in which its author regarded the world of Renaissance story as an opportunity for lyrical treatment. That he was right in claiming for the play a greater inwardness than is found in the *Comedy of Errors* and the *Taming of the Shrew* I doubt. The new kind of verse occurs, naturally, in the scenes of pathos and especially in those where

[1] *Narrative and Dramatic Sources of Shakespeare*, vol. I (London, 1957), pp. 210–11.

Julia, the play's most pathetic figure, is present. But, as if to make it the chief thing in the play, Shakespeare introduces it in the first scene of all. This is not inappropriate, because its main substance is Proteus's sentimental passion for his Julia. The mark of this new verse is a self-conscious creation of verbal music, whether by frequent repetitions of the same word or an extreme range of vowel sounds. Take Valentine's account of what it is like to be in love and the subsequent conversation:

Val. To be in love—where scorn is bought with groans,
    Coy looks with heart-sore sighs, one fading moment's mirth
    With twenty watchful, weary, tedious nights;
    If haply won, perhaps a hapless gain;
    If lost, why then a grievous labour won;
    However, but a folly bought with wit,
    Or else a wit with folly vanquished.
Pro. So, by your circumstance, you call me fool.
Val. So, by your circumstance, I fear you'll prove.
Pro. 'Tis love you cavil at; I am not Love.
Val. Love is your master, for he masters you;
    And he that is so yoked by a fool,
    Methinks, should not be chronicled for wise.
Pro. Yet writers say, as in the sweetest bud
    The eating canker dwells, so eating love
    Inhabits in the finest wits of all.
Val. And writers say, as the most forward bud
    Is eaten by the canker ere it blow,
    Even so by love the young and tender wit
    Is turn'd to folly, blasting in the bud,
    Losing his verdure even in the prime,
    And all the fair effects of future hopes.

                           (I, i, 29)

There is a sense of extreme leisure about these lines. The substance is so sparse that it does not prevent us dwel ling on the music. The alexandrine of the second line and the many repetitions cooperate in creating this sense of leisure. And this sense was Shakespeare's way of rendering in verse the unstinted and drawn out evolution of plot in the prose romance; and like so much of the matter of the romances the object of the passage is not to arouse serious passions but to entertain. This type of verbal music is new in Shakespeare; it is not found in the *Errors* or the *Shrew*: and that novelty becomes especially evident when we compare a passage like the one just quoted with another passage in the *Two Gentlemen*, where action, not sentiment, dominates and the verse is the ordinary norm as found in many passages of the *Errors* or of *Henry VI*. This is the beginning of the Duke's second speech in Act III, thanking Proteus for having betrayed his friend's plan to elope with Silvia:

> Proteus, I thank thee for thine honest care,
> Which to requite, command me while I live.
> This love of theirs myself have often seen,
> Haply when they have judg'd me fast asleep,
> And oftentimes have purpos'd to forbid
> Sir Valentine her company and my court;
> But, fearing lest my jealous aim might err
> And so, unworthily, disgrace the man,
> A rashness that I ever yet have shunn'd,
> I gave him gentle looks, thereby to find
> That which thyself hast now disclos'd to me.
> (III, i, 22)

This direct competence is far from the elaborate patterning of the talk between Valentine and Proteus. It continues an established habit, while the patterning is new, looking forward above all to the most lyrical parts of *Richard II*. For instance, this piece of conversation of

Richard's unhappy queen with her ladies comes very close to the lyrical pathos of parts of the *Two Gentlemen*:

Lady. Madam, we'll tell tales.
Queen. Of sorrow or of joy?
Lady.   Of either, madam.
Queen. Of neither, girl:
      For if of joy, being altogether wanting,
      It doth remember me the more of sorrow;
      And if of grief, being altogether had,
      It adds more sorrow to my want of joy;
      For what I have I need not to repeat,
      And what I want it boots not to complain.
                              (*Richard II*: III, iv, 10)

Here is the same extreme leisure, procured partly by the two incomplete lines, and the same sparseness of matter allowing unhurried attention to the manner of utterance.

But, just as, in describing Felismena's feelings when acting as broker between her Felix and Celia, Montemayor could charge artifice with passion: so there are times when Shakespeare could better the conversation between Proteus and Valentine. The second scene of Act I, derived from Montemayor, describing Julia's dealings with Proteus's letter is about as artificial a piece of writing as you could find. Yet it first touches light comedy and in the end infuses some true feeling into the conventionality of Julia's passion. She has torn the letter up, and now, remorseful at her cruel act, she scans the pieces and pounces on those where her name and his are written.

And here is writ 'love-wounded Proteus'.
Poor wounded name! my bosom, as a bed,
Shall lodge thee till thy wound be throughly heal'd
And thus I search it with a sovereign kiss.
But twice or thrice was 'Proteus' written down.

Be calm, good wind, blow not a word away
Till I have found each letter in the letter—
Except mine own name; that some whirlwind bear
Unto a rugged, fearful, hanging rock,
And throw it thence into the raging sea.
Lo, here in one line is his name twice writ:
'Poor forlorn Proteus, passionate Proteus,
To the sweet Julia'. That I'll tear away;
And yet I will not, sith so prettily
He couples it to his complaining names.
Thus will I fold them one upon another;
Now kiss, embrace, contend, do what you will.

(I, ii, 113)

However elegant and fanciful this may be, the innocent
sensuality of the last lines rises above mere elegance.

But the passage that rises to the strongest feeling is
that in IV, iv, after Proteus has gone out leaving to Julia
the ring she once gave him, to be passed on to Silvia.
First Julia soliloquizes in the patterned manner I have
already referred to:

Alas, poor fool, why do I pity him
That with his very heart despiseth me?
Because he loves her, he despiseth me;
Because I love him, I must pity him.
This ring I gave him, when he parted from me,
To bind him to remember my good will;
And now am I, unhappy messenger,
To plead for that which I would not obtain,
To carry that which I would have refus'd,
To praise his faith, which I would have disprais'd.
I am my master's true confirmed love,
But cannot be true servant to my master
Unless I prove false traitor to myself.

(IV, iv, 89)

Then Silvia enters and she and the supposed page of Proteus talk about him and his abandoned love. Silvia asks Sebastian (for this is the name Julia has assumed) whether he had known Proteus's Julia. He answers: yes, very well. Silvia inquires about Julia's looks, and the scene proceeds as follows:

> *Jul.* She hath been fairer, madam, than she is.
>   When she did think my master lov'd her well,
>   She, in my judgement, was as fair as you;
>   But since she did neglect her looking-glass
>   And threw her sun-expelling mask away,
>   The air hath starv'd the roses in her cheeks
>   And pinch'd the lily-tincture of her face,
>   That now she is become as black as I.
> *Sil.* How tall was she?
> *Jul.* About my stature; for at Pentecost,
>   When all our pageants of delight were play'd,
>   Our youth got me to play the woman's part,
>   And I was trimm'd in Madam Julia's gown;
>   Which served me as fit, by all men's judgements,
>   As if the garment had been made for me;
>   Therefore I know she is about my height.
>   And at that time I made her weep agood,
>   For I did play a lamentable part.
>   Madam, 'twas Ariadne passioning
>   For Theseus' perjury and unjust flight;
>   Which I so lively acted with my tears
>   That my poor mistress, moved therewithal,
>   Wept bitterly; and would I might be dead
>   If I in thought felt not her very sorrow.
>
> (IV, iv, 145)

Of course Julia's account of herself as acting Ariadne is fiction, but it serves to transfer our imaginations from an unnatural world of elegance to one of real happenings;

and the run of the verse corroborates that transfer. This is the point in the play where our feelings are most deeply stirred.

It is perfectly appropriate that the other place which arouses our feelings (of however different a kind) most successfully should closely correspond with the place just discussed. The first line of Julia's soliloquy is, 'How many women would do such a message?' (IV, iv, 86), and it echoes Launce's cry, after describing what he has suffered in protecting his dog, Crab, 'How many masters would do this for his servant?' Of course it is Crab who is really master and Launce who is servant; and while Crab's many outrages correspond to those of Proteus, Launce's patience of insults corresponds to Julia's. Launce and his dog have established themselves so firmly in the affections of readers of Shakespeare that it is hard to believe that they are practically confined to two passages: that just referred to and the account of Launce's leaving his family to go to Milan, in II, iii. This earlier scene is fanciful fooling of a high order and it describes the extremities of tearfulness to which his family is reduced and the contrasting impassivity of Crab:

> My mother weeping, my father wailing, my sister crying, our maid howling, our cat wringing her hands . . . yet did not this cruel-hearted cur shed one tear. He is a stone, a very pebble-stone.
>
> (II, iii, 5)

And Launce goes on to illustrate the scene of parting by a diagram, with his two shoes for father and mother, his stick for his sister, and his hat for the maid. And he reinforces the basic fancy of the diagram by fancy of detail. His mother must be the shoe 'with the worser sole', and of course she thereby indicates a pun and the medieval dispute on whether the woman's soul was equal or inferior to a man's, even whether she had one at all. And when Launce says his sister may aptly be compared to his stick, 'for she is white as a lily and as small as a wand', he is glancing at the heroines of medieval romance or ballad. In its prose way this soliloquy of Launce is as elegant and fanciful as Valentine's opening talk with Proteus or Julia tearing the letter and repenting the act. The other scene, giving samples of Crab's behaviour, assumes an air of greater actuality. Indeed, in the passage about to be quoted, we get the only indication of domestic actuality in the play. I have noted the substantiality of Shakespeare's Ephesus in the *Comedy of Errors* and of Petruchio's country house in the *Taming of the Shrew*. But the rooms where Valentine and Proteus, Julia and Lucetta converse in Verona and the Duke's palace in Milan (in spite of its tower where Silvia was locked in of nights) are about as substantial as the journey by water from Verona to Milan. But when Launce describes how Crab behaved in the Duke's palace, the setting is focused into vivid, if transitory life; and we imagine ourselves within the hall of the palace at dinner time:

> He thrusts me himself into the company of three or four gentlemanlike dogs under the Duke's table; he had not been there, bless the mark, a pissing while but all the table smelt him. 'Out with the dog' says one; 'What cur is that?' says another: 'Whip him out' says the third; 'Hang him up' says the Duke. I, having been acquainted with the smell before, knew it was Crab, and goes me to the fellow that whips the dogs. 'Friend,' quoth I, 'You mean to whip the dog'. 'Ay, marry do I,' quoth he. 'You do him the more wrong;' quoth I. ''Twas I did the thing you wot of.' He makes me no more ado, but whips me out of the chamber. How many masters would do this for his servant?

(IV, iv, 13)

I do not suppose Shakespeare consciously intended it, but this greater vividness of setting corresponds to the nearer approach to a real happening in the lines when Julia feigns herself taking the part of Ariadne in a play. Thus the scenes of Launce and his dog counterpoint those parts of the play that Shakespeare took from Montemayor.

iii. THE PRINCIPLE OF THE CORRECTIVE

In his comedies Shakespeare (I conjecture more by instinct than deliberation) never allowed any dominant theme or motive to remain pure or uncorrected; he was the steady enemy of what Paul Elmore More called the demon of the absolute. He agreed with his Portia that, 'Nothing is good, I see, without respect.' It is the true comic principle because, in life, it helps men to live together in societies, just as the unswerving and uncompromising sticking to a specialized line of conduct makes men difficult to fit in with their fellows. Examples of how Shakespeare acted on this principle of the corrective are abundant. Thus in the *Comedy of Errors* he crossed his fundamental farce by a romantic theme. He knew that motives were mixed, that appearance and reality were apt to be at odds and he insisted that no one thing must remain unchecked and uncountered. So in the *Taming of the Shrew* he crossed the full-blooded story of wife-taming with a thin, elegant, Classico-Italianate piece of convention. Even in details we see the same method. *A Midsummer Night's Dream* ends in the pure goodwill of the fairies blessing the sleeping house; but not till Puck has supplied the anticipatory counterpoise:

> Now the wasted brands do glow,
> Whilst the screech-owl, screeching loud,

Puts the wretch that lies in woe
In remembrance of a shroud.

(*A Midsummer Night's Dream*: V, i, 364)

It was from a deep-seated instinct that Shakespeare was forced to put the bird of ill omen so near his benediction. In the *Merchant of Venice* he crosses the fairy success-story with the sinister figure of Shylock, while in *Twelfth Night* Malvolio's embittered cry of vengeance adulterates the pure gaiety of the ending.

By bearing this principle in mind, we may be able to conjecture with some show of plausibility why Shakespeare behaved so strangely when he dealt with the theme of friendship. We may take it as axiomatic that he could not allow the elegant pathos prompted by Montemayor to remain quite paramount and uncorrected. He did something in this direction by making Launce and his dog comic counterparts of the most pathetic portions of the Julia-Proteus theme. But they were too slight to complete the process, and a more substantial addition to the Montemayor plot, crossing it in spirit, was required. Now to move from the sentiment of love to that of friendship is a natural process; but, having made it, Shakespeare had to avoid the obvious risk of allowing its pathetic possibilities to echo and thus merely to reinforce the very things he intended to cross and counter. If, after the pattern of Titus, Proteus had had a sensitive conscience and suffered bitter remorse at having fallen in love with Silvia, his lamentations over his misfortune might have been too like those of Julia over her lover's desertion. Shakespeare's way out was to blacken Proteus, and thereby he certainly crossed the dulcet strains of Julia's pathos. But he overdid the blackening and thereby failed to make him artistically credible.

It will be apt here to mention one of the most interesting expositions of the *Two Gentlemen*, that of John Vyvyan in his *Shakespeare and the Rose of Love*,[1] if only because my last paragraph is so alien to his own method. Indeed he indicates that difference plainly enough when he writes that he is 'only concerned with trying to establish what Shakespeare aimed at; to estimate the extent of his success in making the audience appreciate these aims is a different matter'. If he is first concerned with aims, I am concerned with how the play presents itself to audience or reader, and with aims only in so far as they help to explain an impression that baffles or seems to be inconsistent. Vyvyan thinks that the *Two Gentlemen* presents, not necessarily with much dramatic success, a closely interlocked allegory of the principles that should govern the actions of love and friendship in a man's mind. H. B. Charlton had already noticed the likenesses between the *Two Gentlemen* and the *Romance of the Rose* in his *Shakespearian Comedy*[2] but Vyvyan develops these in greater detail adding the influence of the Platonism of the Renaissance. Valentine is the pilgrim lover, who begins in the correct manner of exaggerated dedication, errs when he would deceive the Duke and tries to elope with his daughter, is subjected to and survives a period of penance, and emerges into a redeemed state of mind in which the claims of love and friendship no longer conflict. Proteus, young and unstable, but not fundamentally vicious, betrays his friend but is redeemed by the constancy of that friend and the fidelity of Julia who is an allegory of love in one of its aspects. Silvia too is such an allegory in another. Launce and his dog closely parallel the relations of Julia and Proteus. This bare account

[1] pp. 98 ff.   [2] London, 1938, p. 28.

SHAKESPEARE'S EARLY COMEDIES

does not do justice to the ingenuity and plausibility of Vyvyan's thesis. Like his other attempts to see in Shakespeare's plays a highly schematized and constantly recurrent pattern of thought, I find it to mix truth and falsehood. It teaches us the truth that we must be prepared for anything in Shakespeare but at the same time by the very neatness of its findings substitutes a contradicting certainty. To take an example: Valentine's sin in deceiving the Duke. Vyvyan, as I have said, sees this as an episode in a scheme of his mental development, and in a sense I think he is right. But I distrust the very completeness of his scheme. I should say that the terms in which Valentine describes his new love to Proteus, the gratuitous way in which he bullies him on the inferiority of his Julia to Silvia, show a crudeness and a lack of balance in him that dramatically demand punishment and puts us in the right frame of mind for the great scene when the Duke shows up and banishes Valentine. But Vyvyan connects Valentine's deception with the *Romance of the Rose* and the scheme of love's progress therein presented. It is a case of Valentine's enlisting the help of False Semblant. Vyvyan admits that often in Shakespeare the young are justified in rebelling against the old and adds: 'but laudable rebellion is a fine art, and it does not extend to elaborate deception and multitude of lies', such as Valentine was guilty of. Here I ask: what of Lorenzo and Jessica? Surely the deception they practised on Shylock was elaborate, and the number of lies Jessica told her father great? And not only did she deceive her father but she stole his jewels. And yet there is no hint in the play that the pair's actions were sinful. The moral is that it is dangerous to treat Shakespeare cross-sectionally, to expect a consistent scheme running through the whole series. To demand consistency within a play is reasonable: when you pass to the series you must alter your demands and be ready for anything. Then we may follow Vyvyan in thinking that Valentine's experiences in the green wood was educative, and that his fidelity to Silvia, while there, shows him succeeding in an ordeal. But when he demands a precise allegorical meaning for the outlaws as the wild passions of the mind which it is Valentine's duty to keep in control, I am not convinced, even if I admire his ingenuity in citing as parallel the 'rebel powers', which in Sonnet 146 'array the poor soul, the centre of my sinful earth'.

Again Vyvyan, right in his general notion that there are parallels between Proteus and Crab, Julia and Launce, imposes on these a precise scheme:

> Crab is little better than 'ingrateful man'—and, incidentally, most undoglike. His resemblance to Proteus is remarkable. Proteus, too, in his present phase, is being 'a dog in all things', he, too, has thrust himself into the company of gentlemanlike dogs around the duke's table, and misbehaved there; and he would have stolen more from Silvia, had he been able, than a capon's leg. 'O, 'tis a foul thing when a cur cannot keep himself in all companies!' But there must be something about Crab and Proteus that is lovable and worth saving.[1]

Here, to begin with, we are in the realm of attractive options, well worth presenting. But the final comparison sacrifices all fidelity to the text to a preconceived scheme. There is nothing lovable about Shakespeare's Crab, though there is an exquisitely ludicrous fantasy in the relations between him and his master; and to approximate Crab and the notion of salvation is to debit Shakespeare with a wildly inept piece of solemnity. Dramatically

[1] Op. cit., p. 129.

131

we have not the least concern with any possible changes in Crab's future way of life. Proteus, as a man, was theoretically worth saving; but Shakespeare so contrived it that when he is saved salvation is the last thing that the spectator feels is, just then, appropriate.

I do not mean by all this that there can be no recurrent themes within a series of plays; or that we must not expect detailed correspondences in a single play. Only they must be subservient to what the text as living drama indicates.

iv. ANTICIPATIONS

Geoffrey Bullough[1] has remarked that the *Two Gentlemen* is a 'dramatic laboratory in which Shakespeare experimented with many of the ideas and devices which were to be his stock-in-trade and delight for years to come'. This is very true, and critics have cited many resemblances between this and other plays of Shakespeare. It is always possible that Bullough's remark may have a wider significance, helping to explain the dissatisfaction we feel with the play as a work of art. If Shakespeare's main object was to experiment, he may have been deliberately careless of coherence and unity, aiming first at a lively diversity of parts. The hypothesis is remote but just worth mentioning; and I prefer to go on to two instructive resemblances that I have not seen noted before.

Most of the resemblances noted have been between situations or merely objects: Julia, disguised as a page and used by her master to plead with his reluctant mistress, anticipates Viola, Valentine's ladder Romeo's. But the anticipations I have in mind are of whole scenes. The first (III, i) shows the unmasking of Valentine by the Duke. It

[1] Op. cit., p. 210.

begins with Proteus betraying to the Duke that Valentine
is about to elope with his daughter and will be passing
shortly, carrying the rope ladder necessary for the deed.
All that the plot required here was that the Duke should
confront Valentine, unmask him, and send him into exile.
But Shakespeare decided that here was an opportunity for
a big scene and proceeded to elaborate. So he makes
Proteus beg the Duke to choose an oblique method:

> But, good my lord, do it so cunningly
> That my discovery be not aimed at;
> For love of you, not hate unto my friend,
> Hath made me publisher of this pretence.
>
> (III, i, 44)

These are four lines of high dramatic efficiency, for they
both motivate an elaborate scene and add to the meanness
that Shakespeare insists on attaching to Proteus's character. Not only does Proteus not love his former friend, but
he intends to play on the Duke the very trick he says he is
revealing out of love for him. On Valentine's entry, the
Duke feigns ignorance of his plans and proceeds to draw
him out by asking his advice over a problem remarkably
like the present one of how to get away with Silvia.
Valentine, young, inexperienced, and intent on his own
plans, falls into the trap and is most communicative, until
the Duke has the chance of examining Valentine's cloak
and of discovering under it the ladder and a sonnet addressed to his daughter, upon which the banishment
follows. The scene, though unnecessarily drawn out for
the purposes of the play, is superbly dramatic, a perfect
gift to actors with any command of facial expression, with
Valentine of schoolboy aspect giving himself away and the
Duke glowering ferociously behind a superficial mask of
good humour. Its most obvious progeny is the scene in

the *Winter's Tale* where Polixenes and Camillo in disguise attend the shearers' feast, hear Florizel and Perdita innocently reveal their loves, and then unmask, in preparation for Polixenes's pronouncing sentence. Where the later scene differs is in its relation to the whole play. It may be drawn out but it serves the play's purpose in convincing us of the depth and the beauty of the loves of Florizel and Perdita. The earlier scene does indeed seem an isolated experiment: thrilling in itself yet curiously disappointing through not being followed up.

My second instance of anticipation is too obvious to need dwelling on. The part of IV, ii, where Julia and the host watch Proteus's infidelity in courting Silvia leads to the scene in *Troilus and Cressida* where Troilus and Ulysses watch Cressida's infidelity in encouraging the courtship of Diomede. But this later scene from the *Two Gentlemen* differs from the scene of the unmasking of Valentine in that it promotes the play's action substantially; it also differs through belonging to the parts of the action that derive from Montemayor: a combination of facts that strengthen my opinion that from Montemayor Shakespeare took off.

v. CONCLUSION

Of all Shakespeare's comedies the *Two Gentlemen of Verona* gives the dimmest general impression. It does not belong conspicuously to any of the modes which, in my introduction, I grouped within the literary kind popularly called comedy. It does not deal with man's relations with his neighbours and his obligations to society but confines itself to his relations with one, or not more than two, other people. It has nothing to do with farce. Although it con-

tains a rogue as one of its main characters it touches
neither kind of picaresque; for Proteus is neither the
underdog who gets into trouble and wins our sympathy,
nor the engaging rogue whose misdeeds we covertly
applaud. It is only with romance that the play has the
least affinity. There are enough incidents and surprising
turns of fortune to arouse our sense of the marvellous,
but these make no pretence to paramount importance and
fail to give the play any distinctive character. In their
ways the fortunes of Valentine and Julia are success-
stories through an ordeal; and yet Shakespeare fails to
give them the clarity and the power necessary for them to
dominate the whole play. He dwells so lightly on Valentine's period of probation in the forest that it is only with
hesitation that we describe it as such, while his Julia is
vague in character compared with her original in the *Diana
Enamorada*. Still, our best chance of getting any other
than a blurred impression is to give as much heed as
possible to the things Shakespeare derived from Montemayor.

I do not think you will establish any dramatic unity by
detecting pervasive themes. I would agree with Lüthi
that the play contains the theme of the finding of the self,
but it is not coloured or flavoured by it. You do not notice
it powerfully in consecutive reading or witnessing but
have to pick it out by detailed scrutiny in the study. It is
more profitable to seek possible unity through dwelling
on technique. Shakespeare marshals the items of his plot
with great skill, even if he develops those items with very
fluctuating success, and I believe he enjoyed exercising
that skill. In the same way he enjoyed creating a new
kind of blank verse, and, in Launce's soliloquies, a
more flexible kind of prose. Artists of all kinds are more

interested in the details of their craft than are their critics; and it may be that Shakespeare himself was more satisfied with the *Two Gentlemen of Verona* than the critics who have failed to take its technical side much into account.

Chapter VI

LOVE'S LABOUR'S LOST

No play is more discouraging initially than *Love's Labour's Lost* for the kind of reader to whom this book is principally addressed, namely the intelligent amateur with some, but not a professional, knowledge of Shakespeare's work. He will recognize the great quantity of topical allusion in the play and feel he ought to learn something about it. If he painfully hunts it out in an annotated edition he will be held up constantly and find consecutive reading difficult. If he transfers his attention from verbal subtleties to the larger matter of persons—does A in the play stand for B in real life? etc.— he will find himself in a realm of conjecture more uncertain and bewildering than anywhere else in Shakespeare. Take, for instance, the School of Night, theories about which include the identification of Armado with Raleigh. To begin with, critics dispute whether there was such a thing as the School of Night at all; and the dispute centres on the few lines in which the mention occurs, and within them on a single comma, whether or not it is to be regarded. The passage occurs in IV, iii, after the four members of the Academe have admitted that they are in love with the four Frenchwomen. Berowne has been praising his dark-eyed Rosaline and calls for a book, on which he may take an oath:

137

SHAKESPEARE'S EARLY COMEDIES

> That I may sweare Beauty doth beauty lacke,
> If that she learne not of her eye to looke:
> No face is fair that is not full so blacke.
>
> (IV, iii, 247, Folio text)

I take the first two lines to mean that the idea of Beauty, or possibly Venus herself, is imperfect in beauty if it (or she) does not take as the model of its (or her) eyes the black eyes of Rosaline. To this the King of Navarre retorts:

> O paradoxe, Blacke is the badge of hell,
> The hue of dungeons, and the Schoole of night:
> And beauties crest becomes the heavens well.
>
> (IV, iii, 250, Folio text)

The doubt in these lines is: in what does the paradox consist? Does it ratify and enlarge on the paradox of *fair* and *black* in Berowne's last line, or does the King's *paradox* mean simply *nonsense* and his other words enlarge on that meaning? A very close student of Shakespeare's text and a great authority on Elizabethan rhetoric, T. W. Baldwin, thinks the former. He also gives great value to the comma in the second line, making it indicate a balance and a contrast between its two parts. But let him speak for himself, to show what the reader of *Love's Labour's Lost* lets himself in for when he begins to wrestle with the text conscientiously:

Biron had said of Rosaline 'No face is fair that is not full so black.' This black-fair paradox of beauty the King then puts into further contrast in full technical form. The major contrast is between hell and heaven. While black is the 'badge' of hell, it is the 'beauty's crest' of heaven. Here is the major parallel-perpendicular paradox, pointed fully by the technical structure. But this 'beauty's crest becomes the heavens well' only at night. So 'beauty's crest' is Rosaline's black hair on the one hand, and night

138

crowning the heavens on the other. Consequently, the end of the
second line carries over into the paradox of the third line as 'black
night'. Therefore the epithet applied to night in the second line
must have been the equivalent of black. But it is also part of the
triplicity leading from the first line. Black is the 'badge' of hell,
the 'hue' of dungeons, and the '——' of night.[1]

Thus, Baldwin joins the substantial body of critics who
believe the word 'Schoole' to be corrupt and have offered
emendations. He himself plumps for 'shade', partly on the
ground that in this highly rhetorical structure 'just as
badge and crest pair, so do hue and this missing word'.
I spare the reader the alternative explanations of the
'paradox', which can be conveniently found in the excellent new Arden edition of the play. My present point
is that the kind of reader I have in mind can have little
inducement to pursue the topic of the School of Night
when some grave authorities doubt its very existence.

And even if it did exist, being identical with Raleigh's
'School of Atheism', it is far from clear that Armado
stands for Raleigh. The latest book including this topic,
Robert Gittings's *Shakespeare's Rival*,[2] repudiates the
Raleigh-Armado theory and substitutes something highly
ingenious, possibly true, but for the ordinary intelligent
reader even more daunting: namely that Armado in the
original form of the play stood for the exiled Spaniard,
Periz and in its revised form for the 'rival poet', Gervase
Markham.

Such is men's interest in Shakespeare that it is perfectly natural for scholars to try to find out all possible
facts about his intentions. But, luckily for the common
reader, many of these facts have a minimal bearing on his

[1] Shakespeare's Five-Act Structure, pp. 601–2.
[2] London, 1960, chaps. VII and VIII.

appreciation of the play; and the identification of Armado is one of these. Armado is an extravagance who lives because his setting is as extravagant as himself; related to a breathing, three-dimensional, human being in real life, he shrivels into nothing. He can be related to a stock type in conventional Italianate comedy, the Braggart Soldier,[1] to a specially and absurdly stylized type of Elizabethan rhetoric and to an eternal manifestation of human neurosis. Peacock's Scythrop in *Nightmare Abbey* provides a good analogy with Armado. He is known to be a skit on Shelley; but he has the flimsiest relation with Shelley in the flesh; and our appreciation of him as a character in a novel would not be diminished one tittle if we were ignorant of the skit. I do not deny that if the Elizabethan audience could have identified Armado with someone much in the public eye and much subjected to gossip they would have got a pleasure not to be recaptured by a later reader; but that pleasure would consist in a mere reminder of something on which they were amused to dwell, not in any cross-fertilization between the actual man and the character in the play; a pleasure, in fact, we can dispense with at little cost to our total appreciation of the play. The same is true of such a thing as Moth's reference to the dancing horse in II, i. Banks's performing horse, Morocco, was famous for years, and a reference to him must have had a flavour which we shall never recapture. But the loss is not great, for such an animal has a generic as well as a local significance. The animal of almost human intelligence is a recurring phenomenon; and Moth's example links up in our mind with the learned pig in Wordsworth's account of Bartholemew

---

[1] If Shakespeare was responsible for the frequent headings of *Brag* (= *Braggart*) instead of *Arm*. it looks as if he himself agreed.

Fair and with any other freak-animal that our own experience has provided from fair or circus. And the generic significance matters more than the local one.

Thus it is that though the proportion of things the common reader must remain ignorant of, and of things which, even when known, cannot be relished with contemporary zest, is larger in *Love's Labour's Lost* than in any play of Shakespeare, he need not be too alarmed. *Love's Labour's Lost*, after many years of neglect, has been found to act beautifully; and in a performance either the unrewarding topicalities are cut or they pass by so quickly that the spectator is not tempted to dwell on them. And such theatrical experience points to the right method of reading; which is not to be too curious of things plainly irrecoverable but to reserve energies for things more rewarding, which, after all, greatly preponderate.

And when I speak of rewarding things, I have in mind not just the kind of witticism that we can relish as much as the Elizabethans, like this one:

> *Armado.* What great men have been in love?
> *Moth.* Hercules, master.
> *Armado.* Most sweet Hercules! More authority, dear boy, name more; and, sweet my child, let them be men of good repute and carriage.
> *Moth.* Samson, master; he was a man of good carriage: great carriage, for he carried the town gates on his back like a porter; and he was in love.

(I, ii, 63)

Much more than a passage like this I have in mind the larger human strains that coexist with all the quaint and singular affectations with which the play seems mainly to deal. I will illustrate by a strain which, as far as I know, has either been missed or insufficiently developed. And in so illustrating I pass from the play's trimmings to the play itself.

ii. THE MOCKING OF THE MALE ADOLESCENCE

Navarre and his three companions, immediately after they have admitted to being seriously in love and to have broken their vows for love's sake, decide to entertain and hence to woo the objects of their affection with 'some strange pastime';

> For revels, dances, masks, and merry hours,
> Forerun fair Love, strewing her way with flowers.
>
> (IV, iii, 375)

Soon after, Boyet, having had the unexpected fortune to overhear the young men, reports their progress to the women. I quote the whole speech, which, incidentally, the critics agree to pass over in silence.

> Under the cool shade of a sycamore
> I thought to close mine eyes some half an hour;
> When, lo, to interrupt my purpos'd rest,
> Toward that shade I might behold addrest
> The King and his companions; warily
> I stole into a neighbour thicket by,
> And overheard what you shall overhear
> That, by and by, disguis'd they will be here.
> Their herald is a pretty knavish page,
> That well by heart hath conn'd his embassage.
> Action and accent did they teach him there;
> 'Thus must thou speak' and 'thus thy body bear',
> And ever and anon they made a doubt
> Presence majestical would put him out;
> 'For', quoth the king, 'an angel shalt thou see;

Yet fear not thou, but speak audaciously'.
The boy replied, 'An angel is not evil;
I should have fear'd her had she been a devil'.
With that all laugh'd, and clapped him on the shoulder,
Making the bold wag by their praises bolder.
One rubb'd his elbow, thus, and fleer'd, and swore
A better speech was never spoke before.
Another, with his finger and his thumb
Cried 'Via! we will do't, come what will come'.
The third he caper'd, and cried 'All goes well'.
The fourth turn'd on the toe, and down he fell.
With that they all did tumble on the ground,
With such a zealous laughter, so profound,
That in this spleen ridiculous appears,
To check their folly, passion's solemn tears.

(V, ii, 89)

In the last two lines one should know that the spleen was
thought to control the faculty of laughter, that *appears* is
the 'northern plural', and that the last line means not that
the tears of true love checked their laughter but that they
laughed till they cried as copiously as if they had experienced a serious sorrow, the tears cutting short their
foolish laughter. Now, these schoolboy antics are the first
news[1] we have of the young men after Berowne has made
his great speech on love: on the way love heightens the
lover's apprehensions,

But love, first learned in a lady's eyes,
Lives not alone immured in the brain,
But with the motion of all elements
Courses as swift as thought in every power,
And gives to every power a double power,
Above their functions and their offices.

(IV, iii, 323)

[1] I do not include the ladies' receipt of gifts and verses in 'news'.

or on the educational and civilizing influence of the love
that women's eyes engender,

> Never durst poet touch a pen to write
> Until his ink were temper'd with Love's sighs;
> O, then his lines would ravish savage ears,
> And plant in tyrants mild humility.
> From women's eyes this doctrine I derive.
> They sparkle still the right Promethean fire;
> They are the books, the arts, the academes,
> That show, contain, and nourish, all the world
>
> (IV, iii, 342)

It is of course always dangerous to use a great set speech
in Shakespeare as evidence for the character of the
speaker, for it may be a piece of extrinsic rhetoric spoken
by someone who has for the moment ceased to be himself and dwindled into no more than a mouth-piece for
the poet's rhetoric. But here, surely Berowne speaks in
character, for Navarre, knowing his glibness of tongue,
singles him out as the one among them to justify their
perjury most convincingly:

> Then leave this chat; and, good Berowne, now prove
> Our loving lawful, and our faith not torn.
>
> (IV, iii 280)

Now if Berowne speaks both in character and as the
representative of all four members of the academe, surely
Shakespeare meant us to reflect on the contrast between
the high sentiments of Berowne's speech and the childish
behaviour of the academicians immediately afterwards.
In other words, these have not made even a beginning
of growing up through having been forced to recognize
that their scheme for an ascetic life has proved a sham. If
you detect this initial inability to learn, you will see them,

as the play proceeds, plunging from one crude male immaturity to another, until the women, who have been watching them with the detached eye of the more sophisticated sex, administer their pungent medicine at the very end of the play. Only then has the educative process been set in motion; and how far it will proceed we are not informed. I say *not informed,* for critics are too prone to assume that though Jack has not his Jill when the play ends he will have her after the probation of a year and a day is complete.

The crudity of the men's behaviour consists mainly in their disregard of what the ladies they are supposed to be courting would themselves desire. They behave in the very opposite way to Ferdinand in the *Tempest,* who, as soon as he meets Miranda, begs 'that you will some good instruction give/How I may bear me here' (*Tempest,* I, ii, 424). But Navarre and his fellows embark on their disguising, and put up Armado to organize a masque at short notice, without the least thought whether or not the ladies have any wish for these things. They have, in fact, made no progress beyond the mere theory of love; Berowne having set it forth in words, and they all having planned gifts, letter-writing, and the two shows on the abstract notion that these are the correct outcome of the theory.

The women get their first intimation of the men's attack on them through gifts and letters. They cannot dream of taking these seriously. The princess disposes summarily of both, setting the tone for the other women's reactions:

> *Prin.* Sweet hearts, we shall be rich ere we depart,
> If fairings come thus plentifully in.

A lady wall'd about with diamonds!
Look you what I have from the loving King.
                              (V, ii, 1)

A small figure encrusted with precious stones was a
common form of jewelry at the time; and the usual word to
describe the encrustation was *garnished*. The princess's
walled about in substitution for the usual word exquisitely
renders her sense of oppression caused by the gift: she
would be as glad to escape that oppression as an erring
nun the wall that is to immure her. Rosaline then asks
her whether anything accompanied the jewelry and she
answers:

> Nothing but this! Yes, as much love in rhyme
> As would be cramm'd up in a sheet of paper
> Writ o' both sides of the leaf, margent and all,
>   (V, ii, 6)

Clearly Navarre has overdone both the gift and letter.
Katherine, who comments next, is more severe, for she
cannot refrain from comparing the present exhibition of
calf-love with a real passion; calling the god of love a
'shrewd unhappy gallow', and recounting what he did to
her sister:

> He made her melancholy, sad, and heavy;
> And so she died.
>   (V, ii, 16)

As to Dumain's verses she describes them as

> Some thousand verses of a faithful lover;
> A huge translation of hypocrisy,
> Vilely compil'd, profound simplicity.
>   (V, ii, 50)

The princess sums up their common opinion by enlarging
on the adage that there is no fool like a learned fool:

> None are so surely caught, when they are catch'd,
> As wit turn'd fool; folly, in wisdom hatch'd,
> Hath wisdom's warrant and the help of school.
> And wit's own grace to grace a learned fool.
>
> (V, ii, 69)

And immediately Boyet enters with his report, to make
the women's estimate even more convincing; after which
they watch the antics of the unsuspecting males, almost
aghast.

There follows the men's visit dressed as Russians,
Boyet's news of which the princess had hardly credited:

> *Prin.* But what, but what, come they to visit us?
> *Boy.* They do, they do, and are apparell'd thus,
>   Like Muscovites or Russians, as I guess.
>
> (V, ii, 119)

They come all ignorant of Boyet's having overheard
them, heralded by Moth and furnished with only the
most conventional of love's gambits. The women have
no difficulty in routing Moth, bringing the men's flowery
openings to earth with a bump, and through their masks
and changed favours ensuring that each man professes
his love to the wrong woman. The men are blind to what
has happened till their next entry. Then they learn that
the women saw through their disguises; and Berowne,
the quickest of the four, vows he will never again court in
affected terms but confine himself to 'russet yeas and
honest kersey noes.' And when they learn they have been
addressing the wrong women the men's humiliation is
complete.

After this defeat and especially after Berowne's self-criticism one might expect the men to begin acting with more discretion and self-consciousness; but any such expectation proves false, for in the pageant of the Nine Worthies, which breaks in on the men's defeat, their behaviour attains to a new degree of crudity. Now Navarre had himself ordered the pageant and was thus in a sense responsible for it; and one cannot help reflecting that Theseus in *A Midsummer Night's Dream* had not ordered the corresponding show of Pyramus and Thisbe and was not under the same obligation towards the actors in it. Yet Theseus, while allowing himself and his company plenty of scope to be witty about the show, never baits the actors. But Navarre and the other three, joined by Boyet, after allowing Costard to escape with credit, proceed to bait the actors with ever-increasing hilarity and then to work up the dog-fight between Costard and Armado. It is an amazing scene and could be made brilliant on the stage if the women's parts are not forgotten. Of the women only the princess speaks; and her few words either encourage the actors or express sympathy with them when humiliated. But they are all far from superfluous, for we must picture them watching with critical amazement the men, who, having made extravagant professions of love a few moments ago, forget the presence of their adored ones and lose themselves utterly in the puerile sport of making a pitiful show more pitiful by baiting the actors in it and putting them off their parts. The women's interchange of looks during this scene offers in itself great dramatic scope. Ironically it is Berowne, who, in spite of having shown some signs of self-criticism before, leads the baiting and grows the most wildly excited in egging Costard on against his opponent. I do not think one need posit any elaborate reason for the crude behaviour of Navarre and his fellows; for instance that they visit on the actors the humiliation they have just undergone at the women's hands. Their behaviour is simply the culmination of a series of puerilities that began with their light-hearted foundation of the academy. They are too resilient and youthful and fundamentally good-natured to harbour a resentment and work it out on others; and their crime is extreme youth and extreme thoughtlessness. And the women know this and, however critical, are prepared to make allowances.

The arrival of Marcade with his announcement of the French king's death not only breaks off the pageant and the duel but cools the spirits of all the persons and forces them to take stock of the situation. In contemplating the play after Marcade's entrance we should remind ourselves that Navarre and his companions were handsome and attractive young men,[1] and that women do not necessarily withhold their hearts from those they ridicule. And after all Navarre was a king. So when the men asseverate the genuineness of their love, the women sagely decide to give them a chance. But their conditions are severe and expressed in terms much more sober than have so far prevailed. The princess demands of Navarre a year's penance for his broken vow in a 'forlorn and naked hermitage' where he will have to endure 'frosts and fasts, hard lodging and thin weeds' (V, ii, 783). Katherine is kinder than the princess. She is prepared to make great allowances for youth and wishes Dumain a beard along with 'faith health and honesty' (V, ii, 812). All he has to do is to remain faithful for a year and then he may claim her.

[1] E.g., Katherine had said of Dumain in her first description of him that he had 'wit to make an ill shape good/And shape to win grace though he had no wit.' (II, i, 59.)

149

Maria follows Katherine, along with the hint to Longaville that he is just an overgrown boy: 'few taller are so
young' (V, ii, 824). Berowne gets the severest sentence.
Rosaline speaks of his 'wounding flouts,/Which you on
all estates will execute/That lie within the mercy of your
wit' (V, ii, 832). And she is doubtless still feeling her
disgust at his behaviour in baiting the actors and egging
on Costard in his ridiculous duel with Armado. And she
reinforces her censure of Berowne by the principle on
which it is founded:

> A jest's prosperity lies in the ear
> Of him that hears it, never in the tongue
> Of him that makes it;
>
> (V, ii, 849)

And so Berowne must spend his wit for a year in a
hospital, seeing if he can make the 'speechless sick' and
'groaning wretches' appreciate it.

It is absolutely fitting that the most critical of the men
and the man hitherto unable to apply that critical gift to
himself, Berowne, should make the final comment:

> *Ber.* Our wooing doth not end like an old play:
> Jack hath not Jill. These ladies' courtesy
> Might well have made our sport a comedy.
> *King.* Come, sir, it wants a twelvemonth an' a day,
> And then 'twill end.
> *Ber.*   That's too long for a play.
>
> (V, ii, 862)

Surely, here is a repetition of the beginning with Navarre
optimistic about his ill-conceived academy and Berowne
sceptical; and we are meant to be left quite in doubt
whether this time Navarre's optimism concerning the
penances, or Berowne's pessimism, will be justified.

When Berowne in the last quotation said *comedy* he meant no more than an action with a happy ending; if he had used the word in a more comprehensive sense, he would not have been telling the truth, for the action I have described falls entirely within the limits of the comic norm. It ridicules callow youth and it measures that callowness by the requirements of social living. Shakespeare was destined to make individual studies of callow youth: in Bertram and in Troilus. But only in this play, through his presenting not one adolescent but a gang of them, does he turn his critical eye on the general phenomenon of adolescence, on the stage of human life so feelingly described by Keats in the preface to *Endymion*, the stage between childhood and maturity,

> in which the soul is in a ferment, the character undecided, the way of life uncertain, the ambition thick-sighted; thence proceeds mawkishness, and all the thousand bitters which . . . men . . . must necessarily taste in going over the following pages.

This general theme is not usually recognized; but it is just because it is there, coexisting and intertwining with the better recognized ridiculing of every kind of popular verbal affectation, that *Love's Labour's Lost* is so rich and satisfying a comedy.

But if Shakespeare shows us youth in need of education into maturity he also shows us the beginnings of the process. It may be that all or some of the four men will fail in their ordeals but they will be different men from those who failed to keep the rules of their academy. The academy was a fraud from the beginning; the falling in love was genuine and the natural thing for men of their age. The asceticisms of the academy were silly; the penances imposed by the women were appropriate. At least the men have been put on the right road; they are in process of education: and the doubt is not of the rightness of the road but of the men's ability to undergo the rigours of the allotted journey.

iii. THE FEAST OF WORDS

Adolescence is the time of life when men are pronest to feast and surfeit on words; and it is apt that Shakespeare should have combined his criticism of rhetoric with his satire on spiritual immaturity. I have deliberately said 'satire' in the one case and 'criticism' in the other; for though he may tolerate spiritual immaturity as inevitable he shows no affection for it, while in criticizing rhetoric he mixes affection with mockery. Linguistically, he did in *Love's Labour's Lost* the sort of thing Joyce did in *Ulysses*, only of course less heavily and deliberately: give specimens of many varieties of contemporary style in moods ranging from *Bravura* to ridicule. And those varieties were of metre as well of language. He can speak in his own voice also. But we must read him with the knowledge that parody, including self-parody, may break in at any time. Even so, the dividing line between parody and the authentic voice will be very difficult to plot.

What, for instance, are we to make of Navarre's speech to the Princess on her political mission?

> Madam, your father here doth intimate
> The payment of a hundred thousand crowns;
> Being but the one half of an entire sum
> Disbursed by my father in his wars.
> But say that he or we, as neither have,
> Receiv'd that sum, yet there remains unpaid
> A hundred thousand more, in surety of the which,

> One part of Aquitaine is bound to us,
> Although not valued to the money's worth.
> If then the King your father will restore
> But that one half which is unsatisfied,
> We will give up our right in Aquitaine,
> And hold fair friendship with his Majesty.
>
> (II, i, 127)

This is solemn and prosaic and unlike the norm of the play in so being. It also resembles the more factual passages in *Henry VI*. Was Shakespeare merely giving in an accustomed manner some information necessary to the progress of the play or was he risking a parody of himself in the faith that the audience would spot and enjoy his joke? And what of the 'witty' passages, consisting of those plays on words some of which we find so deplorably flat? In the best of them there can be no question of parody. This is Costard trying to quibble himself out of the penalty due to him for having been taken in company with Jacquenetta:

> *King.* It was proclaimed a year's imprisonment to be taken with a wench.
> *Cost.* I was taken with none, sir; I was taken with a damsel.
> *King.* Well, it was proclaimed damsel.
> *Cost.* This was no damsel neither, sir; she was a virgin.
> *King.* It is so varied too, for it was proclaimed virgin.
> *Cost.* If it were, I deny her virginity; I was taken with a maid.
> *King.* This 'maid' will not serve your turn, sir.
> *Cost.* This maid will serve my turn, sir.
>
> (I, i, 271)

Reinforced by the two uses of the vocative 'sir', Costard's equivocation goes down well enough, even today. We can accept it as straight Shakespeare. But is parody out of the question when it comes to the more frigid and

far-fetched plays on words, in which *Love's Labour's Lost*,
beyond any other play of Shakespeare, abounds? Take this
example: an interchange of wit between Katherine and
the dark Rosaline at the beginning of V, ii; Katherine tells
Rosaline that she may live to be a grandmother, 'for a light
heart lives long'.

Ros. What's your dark meaning, mouse, of this light word?
Kath. A light condition in a beauty dark.
Ros. We need more light to find your meaning out.
Kath. You'll mar the light by taking it in snuff;
Therefore I'll darkly end the argument.
Ros. Look what you do, you do it still i' th' dark.
Kath. So do not you; for you are a light wench.
Ros. Indeed, I weigh not you; and therefore light.
Kath. You weigh me not? O, that's you care not for me.
Ros. Great reason; for 'past cure is still past care'.
Prin. Well bandied both; a set of wit well play'd.
(V, ii, 19)

Help on the different meanings of the word *light* in this
passage can be found in the masterly brief footnote of the
Arden edition. The passage itself can be paraphrased
somewhat as follows: '*Ros.* What's the hidden meaning
of your trivial remark? *Kath.* A wanton disposition in a
dark beauty. *Ros.* More information is needed to establish
your meaning. *Kath.* As you can spoil the light of a candle
by snuffing it badly, so you will obscure an intended
meaning by getting annoyed. Therefore I will let the
argument lapse into obscurity. *Ros.* Yes indeed, obscurity
is much to the point in your case: when you misbehave
with a man, always see that you keep it secret. *Kath.* A
superfluous precaution for you, for all know the precarious
state of *your* morals. *Ros.* If I'm light, it is because I'm
slimmer and weight less than you. *Kath.* Your words can

154

just as well mean you don't regard me. *Ros.* Quite right, if there is truth in the proverb about "caring and curing".' What are we to make of this very slenderly consequent piece of wit? Did Shakespeare think it was the real right stuff? or did he mean the princess's concluding remark to show that it was a set and deliberate piece of bandying such as was only too common among the bright young people of the time the play was written? I doubt if the question can be answered; and this doubt points to an irreducible minimum of the play's matter for which we can have little use.

It is otherwise with the general targets of Shakespeare's linguistic criticisms. He lived in an age of uncommon proliferation and profusion of words; he welcomed and profited by these things: but he knew that what he welcomed could be abused and he delighted in pointing to the abuses. But before I begin on this main topic I must say something about the variety of metres to which I have already referred.

As Shakespeare extended the range of effects he could achieve through blank verse and prose so he reduced the number of metres he employed. He never rejected the use of exceptional metres for special effects (witness the apparition in *Cymbeline* and the masque in the *Tempest*) but he excluded them from the main action of a play. But in his earlier comedies he could vary blank verse with other metres freely enough at any point in a play. Even in the stately conventionality of his early Histories he was not quite restricted to blank verse, for in the culminating scene of *I Henry VI*, the death of the Talbots, he resorted to couplets. The commonest metres other than blank verse in the earliest comedies are the decasyllabic couplet, quatrains alternately rhymed, and rhymed doggerel.

Love's Labour's Lost differs from the others in containing the smallest proportion of blank verse and the greatest variety of other metres; and, I think, for the same reasons that governed his rhetoric in this play. Where, in the *Comedy of Errors* for instance, he would use doggerel because he thought it appropriate to the speakers and the situation, in *Love's Labour's Lost* he goes beyond mere propriety and either glories in a great variety of metres for its own sake or reviews satirically the metrical fashions of his own or the immediately antecedent day. Take Holofernes's ridiculous lines in IV, ii, on the deer the princess has shot:

The preyful Princess pierc'd and prick'd a pretty pleasing pricket.
Some say a sore; but not a sore till now made sore with shooting.
(IV, ii, 53)

In their pedantic affectation these fit Holofernes; but as well as being normally dramatic Shakespeare here satirizes (and not without nostalgic enjoyment) a habit of excessive alliteration that was going out of fashion. When in IV, iii, the four men find that they are all in love and equally incriminated they speak in a long series of rhymed quatrains; but Shakespeare creates variety by making Berowne introduce them with a stanza of rime royal:

Sweet lords, sweet lovers, O, let us embrace!
  As true we are as flesh and blood can be.
The sea will ebb and flow, heaven show his face;
  Young blood doth not obey an old decree.
We cannot cross the cause why we were born,
Therefore of all hands must we be forsworn.
(IV, iii, 210)

The lyrical stanza suits the heightened sentiment; but it adds yet another sample to the repertory of metres

Shakespeare used in the play: and I believe he enjoyed making that addition. Here are two metrical varieties not found in the other early comedies. In two places, in II, i, occur short passages of rhymed iambic trimeters and anapaestic dimeters.

> *Ber.* What time o' day?
> *Ros.* The hour that fools should ask.
> *Ber.* Now fair befall your mask!
> *Ros.* Fair fall the face it covers!
> *Ber.* And send you many lovers!
> *Ros.* Amen, so you be none.
> *Ber.* Nay, then I will be gone.
>> (II, i, 121. Folio distribution of speakers)

In the other passage Berowne says that he is sick at heart, and the dialogue proceeds:

> *Ros.* Alack, let it blood.
> *Ber.* Would that do it good?
> *Ros.* My physic says 'ay'.
> *Ber.* Will you prick't with your eye?
> *Ros.* No point, with my knife.
> *Ber.* Now, God save thy life!
> *Ros.* And yours from long living!
> *Ber.* I cannot stay thanksgiving.
>> (II, i, 185)

Strangest of all is the end of Act II, where doggerel gives way to regular four-stressed anapaests. This is Boyet describing the symptoms of love in Navarre:

His tongue, all impatient to speak and not see,
Did stumble with haste in his eyesight to be;
All senses to that sense did make their repair,
To feel only looking on fairest of fair.
Methought all his senses were lock'd in his eye,

157

As jewels, in crystal for some prince to buy;
Who, tendring their own worth from where they were glass'd,
Did point you to buy them, along as you pass'd.
His face's own margent did quote such amazes
That all eyes saw his eyes enchanted with gazes.

(II, i, 237)

This passage is indeed strange in Shakespeare but it is less strange in the context of metrical variety, for in that variety he was not being original but was following the precedent of the kind of drama that had been fashionable and whose vogue was just beginning to go out. Anapaests are not common in that drama but they exist, as in *Appius and Virginia*, where, following fourteeners and doggerel, comes this from Virginia:

O father, my comfort! O mother, my joy!
O dear and O sovereign! do cease to employ
Such dolorous talking where dangers are none:
Where joys are attendant what needeth this moan?[1]

The rhymed trimeters I have pointed to can be matched in Lodge's *Wounds of Civil War*. Whetstone's *Promos and Cassandra* contains samples of all the principal metres used in *Love's Labour's Lost*. Many plays to which Shakespeare may have made metrical reference have been lost and few of his modern readers know the surviving early plays well enough to detect imitations or parodies of them. But it would be wrong to deal with the rhetoric of *Love's Labour's Lost* without explaining that Shakespeare's educated contemporaries, and especially the theatre-going aristocrats whose delectation he most had in mind, would have seized on and emphatically relished an abundance of metrical allusion.

---

[1] In *Early English Dramatists: Five Anonymous Plays* (fourth series); ed. John S. Farmer (London, 1908), p. 8, l. 18 ff.

I can now return to my general topic of Shakespeare's
linguistic criticism. It has been finely treated by Miss
G. D. Willcock in her Shakespeare Association pamphlet
for 1934, *Shakespeare as Critic of Language*. She considers
that he was lucky in the date of his birth. He came to
maturity at a time when an unparalleled awareness of
words and rhetoric, beginning in mid-century, was being
civilized by a more critical spirit. There had been an
outburst of sheer linguistic invention, producing an abundance that needed sifting. And now, with the emergence of
a more cultured type of courtier, the civilizing process
had become possible. Shakespeare, having that kind of
courtier in mind, was, among dramatists, the leader in
this process. He used words far more critically than
Peele or Greene or Marlowe. And of all plays *Love's
Labour's Lost* shows him being critical of words and rhetoric
most persistently. Not that Shakespeare was averse to
rhetorical opulence: only it must have a sufficient reason.
It was indeed necessary for dealing with all the phases of
life that interested him. But there was also an opulence
that lacked meaning and whose use was pure affectation.
As Miss Willcock said:

> Shakespeare himself has no objection to neologism and was a
> prolific coiner of words. In Holofernes' and Armado's poly-
> syllabic extravagances he pillories the brand of affectation and
> types of pompous perversity which, as a poet and a man of
> humour, he thought the language could do very well without.

She also makes the important point that the abuses of
language committed by Armado and Holofernes were
current. Armado's 'talk has none of the archaic clichés
of Pistol but exaggerates current fashion'. And again,
'practically every remark of Holofernes is a pointer to

something going on in the world of language'. This truth is especially important because it shows the pedants as parallel to the courtiers. If the courtiers toyed with an up-to-date fragment of ascetic neo-Platonism, Armado and Holofernes affected an up-to-date learning. And if the courtiers showed an obvious adolescence in the frivolous way they entered on their vows, the pedants were as frivolously adolescent in the way they abused the language. The shape of the play gains greatly when we recognize these parallels.

In her pages on *Love's Labour's Lost* Miss Willcock concentrates on the pedants. But it is wrong to confine the verbal criticism to them. I have already pointed to a passage where Shakespeare may be parodying his own style in his earliest Histories; and, if we are to read the play properly, we must be ready for parody at any moment. Take the first speech of Act II, that of Boyet urging the French princess to put up a good show in her embassy to Navarre:

> Now, madam, summon up your dearest spirits.
> Consider who the king your father sends,
> To whom he sends, and what's his embassy:
> Yourself, held precious in the world's esteem,
> To parley with the sole inheritor
> Of all perfections that a man may owe,
> Matchless Navarre; the plea of no less weight
> Than Aquitaine, a dowry for a queen.
> Be now as prodigal of all dear grace
> As Nature was in making graces dear,
> When she did starve the general world beside
> And prodigally gave them all to you.
>
> (II, i, 1)

I cannot believe that this is merely Boyet being very

French and floridly courtly. Surely in the *who, to whom,*
and *what,* followed by an explanation of each in that
order, we are meant to think of Armado in the scene before with his *time when, ground which,* and *place where* and
to detect a satire on a whole area of affected speech. Here
we can be sure enough of the parody; but, whereas with
pedants we know just where we are, with the courtiers we
often have to be content with uncertainty. What, for
instance, are we to make of this speech of Navarre, coming
at a serious point in the play after the appearance of the
messenger of death. In it he urges the princess to allow
unusual conditions to excuse unusual practice, in this
case an unusual speed of decision.

> The extreme parts of time extremely forms
> All causes to the purpose of his speed;
> And often at his very loose decides
> That which long process could not arbitrate.
> And though the mourning brow of progeny
> Forbid the smiling courtesy of love
> The holy suit which fain it would convince,
> Yet, since love's argument was first on foot,
> Let not the cloud of sorrow justle it
> From what it purpos'd; since to wail friends lost
> Is not by much so wholesome-profitable
> As to rejoice at friends but newly found.
>
> (V, ii, 728)

Here I am defeated. At first sight one thinks this cannot
be wholly serious. What a monstrous equivalent for *family
bereavement* is the *mourning brow of progeny,* and what a
monstrous violence of metaphor is contained in *cloud of
sorrow justle it*! And yet, in view of Shakespeare's habit of
inflation all through his career in passages of formal dialogue, I cannot be certain that we have more than Navarre

striving to be stately at a difficult moment. In fact, here we have one of a number of passages whose rhetorical connotations can only remain in doubt.

In one department of rhetoric Shakespeare was not being satirical: that of double meanings. He was one with his fellows in loving these. More often than not they were bawdy; and there is more bawdy equivocation in *Love's Labour's Lost* than in most of the comedies. This is fitting enough, for an audience on the look out for the abuses of language (and for such the play was clearly intended) would be alert to other linguistic curiosities, double meanings included. And the feast of words, once begun, had better be as rich as possible. The quality of the bawdy varies. In IV, iii, after the four Frenchmen have learnt their common perjury and before Berowne says his great speech on love, there is a dialogue on the darkness of his Rosaline. It ends thus. Longaville points to his shoe (presumably black and well polished) and says, 'Look, here's thy love: my foot and her face see.' And the dialogue proceeds:

> *Ber.*   O, if the streets were paved with thine eyes,
>   Her feet were much too dainty for such tread!
> *Dum.*   O vile! then, as she goes, what upward lies
>   The street should see as she walk'd overhead.
>
> (IV, iii, 274)

This is indeed frigid and gratuitous. Berowne's lines may introduce the jest but they have no connection with the sense of what has gone before except the mere pointless echo of *foot* by *feet*. But take these speeches of Nathaniel and Holofernes and what they say about the schoolgirls:

> *Nath.* Sir, I praise the Lord for you, and so may my parishioners; for their sons are well tutor'd by you, and their daughters

profit greatly under you. You are a good member of the commonwealth.

Hol. Mehercle! if their sons be ingenious, they shall want no instruction; if their daughters be capable, I will put it to them;

(IV, ii, 70)

Bearing in mind a possible meaning of *member* and one of the activities in which Hercules excelled, we may hail the ingenuity of the passage, which of course takes its place in the tradition of the innocent unconsciously saying or implying so much more than he intended. Shakespeare exploits the same formula as that embodied in the story of the curate giving out notices: 'And we also propose to revive our Mother's Union. Any ladies wishing to be mothers are invited to meet me in the vestry after the service.' It is a formula that has given wide-spread satisfaction over the ages; and, when Shakespeare exploits it with delicate skill, we can only applaud.

I say nothing about the identification of characters in the play with real people, not only because I lack the special equipment needed for entering this field of battle but because it has next to no bearing on the enjoyment of the play. On the other hand, though it profits little aesthetically to identify or to refuse to identify Gabriel Harvey with one of the play's persons, it profits very much to know the kind of prose he was writing about this time, for it is one of the current kinds that provoked Shakespeare to write as he did. Take this from the third of the *Foure Letters*, directed at Greene and published in 1592:

Right artificiality (whereat I once aimed to the uttermost power of my slender capacity) is not mad-brained or ridiculous or absurd or blasphemous or monstrous, but deep-conceited but pleasurable but delicate but exquisite but gracious but admirable; not according to the fantastical mould of Aretine or Rabelais but according

163

to the fine model of Orpheus, Homer, Pindarus, and the excellentest wits of Greece and of the land that flowed with milk and honey. For what festival hymns so divinely dainty as the sweet psalms of King David, royally translated by Buchanan? or what sage gnomes, so profoundly pithy, as the wise proverbs of King Solomon? notably also translated—but how few Buchanans! Such lively springs of streaming eloquence and such right-Olympical hills of amounting wit I cordially recommend to the dear lovers of the Muses.[1]

And Harvey is but one of many who, feasting on words in their several ways, notably provoked Shakespeare to the writing of *Love's Labour's Lost*.

iv. THE CHARACTERS

Before going on to the motives which I believe to unite the two themes of adolescence and verbal excess, I must say something of the characters. And indeed it is apt to do so just here, for as Armado and Holofernes were the leaders in verbal excess so, for all their subordinate position in the plot, are they the leading characters. To say this is to go against common opinion, which has no doubt that Berowne is the one who stands out from all the others. Apart from Berowne it is thought that the interest in the play lies in words not in character. For instance, Granville-Barker, who admires the play, queries as follows:

> What fresh life can the actors give to this fribble of talk and nice fantasy of behaviour? As satire it means nothing to us now. Where are the prototypes of Armado and Holofernes, Moth and Nathaniel the curate? We can at best cultivate an historical sense of them.[2]

[1] *Foure Letters*, ed. G. B. Harrison (London, 1922), pp. 67–8.
[2] *Prefaces to Shakespeare*, first series (London, 1927), p. 12.

He may be right about Moth, who in the modern world would still be at school and in a totally different relation to his seniors. But Nathaniel in his little way and Armado and Holofernes in their great ways are fresh versions of eternal types. As characters they are far more emphatic than Berowne, for they are clean-cut whereas the very essence of Berowne is an adolescent fluidity. But the topic now demands greater detail.

Berowne is a mouth rather than a formed character. He is naturally eloquent and he is ready with words appropriate to any occasion. The best poetry is put into his mouth. In quickness of apprehension he is always well ahead of his fellows; and his power of self-criticism is his most endearing quality. When the four academicians perceive that in their Russian disguise they have been tricked into courting the wrong women and turn pale, it is Berowne who, touched by Rosaline's cruel and brilliant, 'sea-sick, I think, coming from Muscovy' (V, ii, 393), sees their game is up, throws in his hand, and decides that there is nothing for it but to grovel:

> Thus pour the stars down plagues for perjury.
> Can any face of brass hold longer out?
> Here stand I, lady—dart thy skill at me,
> Bruise me with scorn, confound me with a flout,
> Thrust thy sharp wit quite through my ignorance,
> Cut me to pieces with thy keen conceit;
> And I will wish thee never more to dance,
> Nor never more in Russian habit wait.
> O, never will I trust to speeches penn'd,
> Nor to the motion of a school-boy's tongue,
> Nor never come in vizard to my friend,
> Nor woo in rhyme, like a blind harper's song.
>
> (V, ii, 394)

It is charming eloquence; and Berowne's admission of adolescence ('school-boy's tongue') is engaging. And it is engaging in the same way as his speech at the end of Act III ('And I, forsooth, in love') in which he castigates himself for being such a fool as to fall a victim to the thing he has habitually mocked at. And especially engaging is the way he makes his crime worse by pretending that his Rosaline is a wanton, unworthy of his affections. Of course he knows that she, like the other Frenchwomen, is a model of propriety; and his humorous pretence is entirely at his own expense. Surely John Vyvyan[1] is being heavy-handed when he takes Berowne's strictures on his Rosaline seriously and argues from them that his love was insincere. That love was indeed not deep, for Berowne's character has no depth, but it is sincere as far as it goes. But though Berowne's ready self-criticism is engaging, his chief habit of mind is to go back on or to forget the things he has just professed to mind about. In the first scene, having shown up the Academe for what it is worth, he proceeds to subscribe to its laws. In the scene when the loves of the four academicians are revealed he moralizes severely on the sin of perjury only to go back on his words when shown up. Having uttered superb lines on the all-absorbing sway of love, he joins with the others in oblivious horseplay while prompting Moth as prologue to their disguise. When the men discover that in their disguise they have been addressing the wrong women and Berowne makes his grovelling speech, the beginning of which I have quoted, he ends by forswearing artifice and with the declaration, meant to be the height of honest forthrightness,

---

[1] Op. cit., pp. 34 and 43.

And, to begin, wench—so God help me, law!—
My love to thee is sound, sans crack or flaw.

(V, ii, 414)

And immediately after, in the excitement of baiting the actors in the show of the Nine Worthies and of speeding the duel between Armado and Costard, his love shows a glaring flaw as he forgets his Rosaline and what she is thinking about it all. Whatever he will turn out to be, in the play Berowne has not yet acquired anything that merits the name of character. Nor is the play the worse for the uncertainty: had Berowne possessed more character he would have been of less use in promoting the theme of adolescence.

Armado derives from the braggart soldier of Classical and Renaissance comedy; and we have only to put him alongside the other Shakespearean derivatives, Falstaff and Parolles, to see how brilliantly Shakespeare can diversify an inherited type. Like Parolles he is shown up. The best excuse he can find to avoid the fight with Costard is that, being shirtless, he cannot meet Costard's resolution to strip. But the excuse serves its turn, for it postpones the fight for a few moments until the entry of Marcade interrupts and reverses all the trends of the action. Berowne, hearing the news of the French king's death, tells the actors to be gone: 'Worthies, away; the scene begins to cloud.' But for Armado the opposite is true, and the scene has suddenly cleared:

> For mine own part, I breathe free breath. I have seen the day of wrong through the little hole of discretion and I will right myself like a soldier.

(V, ii, 711)

the last sentence of which the *New Cambridge Shakespeare*

editors paraphrase as, 'I have seen the danger from Costard and have avoided it with a little discretion, which is the better part of valour, as a soldier would say.' But except in the matter of professing martial qualities and being shown up, Armado and Parolles are poles apart. Parolles has no illusions about himself; he is a deliberate and self-acknowledged fraud, out for what he can get. And when the game is up, he makes no plans for renewing it. The very essence of Armado is that he lives in a world of illusion. Miss B. Roesen[1] has written well of his imagined consorting with the great heroes of history and legend, Hercules and Samson and King Cophetua. Thus to consort, and to picture himself the confidant of his own sovereign are the very mainspring of his existence. The pageant of the Nine Worthies amplifies in his mind the kinship he claimed with Hercules and Samson through falling in love. Thus the hooting of Hector off the stage is more than a personal slight; it is a blow at the imagined world he cannot do without. As Miss Roesen put it:

> Armado is a member of the court itself, has had some reason to pride himself upon the King's favor, and has been good enough to arrange the pageant in the first place. The people represented in it are those who inhabit that strange world of his fancy, and one knows that his anguish is not alone for his personal humiliation, but for that of the long-dead hero he portrays, when he cries, 'The sweet war-man is dead and rotten; sweet chucks, beat not the bones of the buried; when he breathed, he was a man.'

How necessary were Armado's illusions to his very existence is shown by his proceeding to fabricate a second as soon as the first collapses. At the very end, after Navarre and the others have been given their penances, Armado

[1] *Shakespeare Quarterly*, 1953, pp. 411–26. References to Armado pp. 415 and 423. I owe a great debt to this admirable essay.

enters, seemingly recovered, and thus addresses the king:

> I will kiss thy royal finger, and take leave. I am a votary: I have
> vowed to Jaquenetta to hold the plough for her sweet love three
> year.

(V, ii, 870)

Deprived of his kinship with Hercules and Samson, he must claim kinship with Jacob wooing his Rachel and hold the plough for three years. Essentially Armado is a naked, unprotected soul who cannot exist without a barrier of pretence between himself and things as they are; and his lack of a shirt symbolizes that nakedness. His fantastically inflated rhetoric, in itself a source of pure delight to the audience, not only satirizes current affectation but worthily renders the clouds or the smoke-screen that poor Armado by his very nature is forced to emit in order to go on living at all.

Thus, far from being a mere vehicle of ridiculous words, Armado is both a unique character and the eternal type of those for whom life is too much and who must somehow erect a barrier against it. Far more than to Parolles he is kin to Malvolio or even Coriolanus. The kinship with Malvolio may readily be granted, that with Coriolanus depends on the interpretation of the Roman's character. And I regard him as a man, naturally brave indeed but driven to joyless and excessive feats of valour to hide the nakedness of his guilt in never having freed his self from the sway of his terrible mother: a nakedness laid bare when in a heart-rending moment near the play's end Aufidius calls him 'boy'. Of course Aufidius meant no more than to be generally abusive; he had no inkling of what connotations the scornful word bore for his enemy. For Coriolanus it is the end of all hope, the compulsion to face what cannot be faced. Armado is built on a smaller scale, and has fewer parts than the other two, but he is none the less an eternal type and one of Shakespeare's great characters.

Even with Sir Nathaniel the Curate, a very minor figure, I think that Granville-Barker's assertion that at best we can cultivate an historical sense of him is mistaken. Surely we all know the meek person, male or female, who has been landed in a position to which he does not quite measure up and who attaches himself for protection to someone stronger. Heaven knows, we comment, how ever Nathaniel got any bishop to ordain him; but we recognize him as perfectly harmless and do not grudge him Holofernes's patronage. And we sympathize with Costard's kind words when, as Alexander the Great, he has been hooted off the scene:

> There, an't please you, a foolish mild man; an honest man, look you, and soon dash'd. He is a marvellous good neighbour, faith, and a very good bowler; but for Alisander—alas! you see how 'tis—a little o'erparted.
>
> (V, ii, 576)

Nathaniel also serves to give stature to his patron, Holofernes, who in his way is a grandiose figure. Holofernes must, we feel, have established a remarkable ascendency over the family of one of his pupils to be able to bring Nathaniel and even Dull along with him to dine. Certainly his invitation to Nathaniel is full of assurance:

> I do dine today at the father's of a certain pupil of mine; where, if, before repast, it shall please you to gratify the table with a grace, I will, on my privilege I have with the parents of the foresaid child or pupil, undertake your ben venuto;
>
> (IV, ii, 144)

His pronouncements on literature are magisterial. We are

not privileged to hear how at the dinner he 'proved those
verses' (that is Berowne's sonnet to Rosaline that went
astray), 'to be very unlearned, neither savouring of poetry,
wit, nor invention'; but we have the comment of Nathaniel
dutifully floundering in imitative wake of his patron, on
the proof:

> I praise God for you, sir. Your reasons at dinner have been sharp
> and sententious; pleasant without scurrility, witty without affec-
> tion, audacious without impudency, learned without opinion,
> and strange without heresy.
>
> (V, i, 2)

And as Judas Maccabaeus in the show of the Worthies,
though in the end put out of countenance by the concerted
hoots of his social betters, Holofernes put up some resis-
tance and even retaliated before leaving the scene: 'This
is not generous, not gentle, not humble,' (V, ii, 620).
There is indeed something tough, even formidable, about
Holofernes. That he was a pedant is obvious; but people
have denied Holofernes his full stature because they confine pedants to the ranks of dons and schoolmasters. I
grant that the philologists, of whom Holofernes was one,
supply their full quota, but I have met pedants among
lawyers, clergymen, regular soldiers, and hospital nurses,
to name only a few classes. Pedantry consists in making
too much of things of small moment; and in its acuter
forms infusing passion into the process. In the first world
war I served as adjutant under a colonel of the regular army
who in one detail was as pedantic as Holofernes. He was a
man of aggressive courage and a most capable officer; but
he was obsessed with a passionate conviction that every
battalion kitchen ought to have a stockpot for its scraps of
food for the making of soup. Doubtless the stockpot was

a sensible idea but in conditions of trench warfare it was not always easy to realize. However, that did not matter. A good battalion was distinguished from a bad by having a stockpot; and a stockpot there must be even if it wallowed in two feet of mud. Holofernes's most passionately held item of pedantic belief was that words should be pronounced as they are spelt: a belief by no means dead and the frequent cause of inherited ways of pronouncing being given up; see, for instance, the B.B.C. habit of calling a conduit a *con-dew-it* and not a *cun-dit*. Armado offended against this principle and incurs Holofernes's most passionate condemnation:

> I abhor . . . such rackers of orthography, as to speak 'dout' fine, when he should say 'doubt'; 'det' when he should pronoune 'debt'—d, e, b, t, not d, e, t. He clepeth a calf 'cauf', half 'hauf'; neighbour vocatur 'nebour'; 'neigh' abbreviated 'ne'. This is abhominable—which he would call 'abbominable'. It insinuateth me of insanie: ne intelligis, domine? to make frantic, lunatic.
>
> (V, i, 17)

Holofernes's principle may sound specialized, peculiar to the academic world, but in basic nature it does not differ from the colonel's stockpot; and Holofernes is the eternal type of pedants of whatever profession, and of the pedantry we all, even if only in the minutest quantity, contain within ourselves. It is legitimate for us to make our own pictures of Shakespeare's characters provided we do not try to impose them on others. I like to picture Holofernes as a man of commanding stature with the glint of fanaticism in his eye and an occasional blink when he grows passionate.

John Vyvyan in his *Shakespeare and the Rose of Love* argues for the influence of the *Romance of the Rose* on three early plays of Shakespeare, *Love's Labour's Lost* being one of them. There is no inherent improbability in his having read the poem in editions of Chaucer; and the theme of love's being an education with its own discipline is indeed common to both. Shakespeare *might* have drawn it from that medieval source. But he could have drawn it just as well from Spenser and Sidney; and when Vyvyan makes the French princess an allegorical figure of Love and Beauty, I am bound to retort that such an identification is at odds with my impression of the play. Like Luciana in the *Comedy of Errors* she is what D. H. Lawrence called a hen-sure woman, but in an aristocratic not a bourgeois setting. She is fully grown up and she knows a great deal about life; and she exists principally to be a foil to the young men who are still so fluid in character and so uncertain of themselves. She serves also to propel them in the direction of being educated. She diffuses a sense of the very best that the aristocratic principle can attain to, but her character is so little developed that she acts more as a function than a person. Nor do we wish her to do more.

V. THE OVERRIDING THEME

Love's Labour's Lost is neither a farce, nor a picaresque play, nor, in spite of the strangeness of the park of Navarre, a fairy play. It belongs, as I have said, to the central area of social comedy. Four young men, refusing to see things as they are, attempt a feat which common sense could have told them was impossible. That impossibility becomes quickly apparent, but even then they persist in their childish vision of reality. But society, in the form of four clear-sighted women, and the unexpected irruption of the reality of death give them a series of lessons and put them on the way to seeing things as they are. Matching the four young men in their distorted vision of reality are two older men and a hanger-on of one of them. One of these distorts reality by clothing his spiritual nakedness in fantasies, and they both violate reality by enlarging the distance of words from the things they represent. They are fully grown and set in their habits and, unlike the young men, who are still malleable, they will continue to be comparatively harmless misfits in the society to which they belong; or, to put their case more accurately in terms of the play, they will remain for ever islanded in that park of Navarre which is made to stand so exquisitely for a state of affairs at odds with what prevails beyond its bounds. Whatever becomes of the four young men, they have, by the end of the play, quitted the old enclosure. In contrast, Armado and Holofernes will inhabit it for ever.

How does Shakespeare fabricate the delicate unreality of the park? Is it through making fantastic things happen there? Or is it through using strange words to denote its attributes, for instance, the afternoon there being the posterior of the day? Or are the items of its furniture studiedly unexpected and incongruous? These include a bench in a manor-house, a 'curious-knotted garden', a dairy (since Jacquenetta was 'allowed for the day-woman' (I, ii, 125)), the 'steep up rising of a hill', a deer, a school, a sycamore: things that make their impression but which do not add up to a district where real life goes on. Whatever the means, Shakespeare makes his park into a kind of Cloudcuckooland and by siting his comic action there creates a most unusual kind of comedy. In normal comedy the folk who trangress the social norm are set within it; in *Love's Labour's Lost* the social norm is a

visitor breaking through the barriers by which Cloudcuckooland is enclosed. This reversal of the usual procedure renders the play unique; and the only fit response is
one of simple admiration for a stroke of genius.

Not that the park is given over entirely to the fantasts,
who could indeed consider their world betrayed by what
is false within in the form of Costard and Jacquenetta.
But these are slight persons; and the Frenchwomen make
the main invasion. Miss Roesen has defined with nice
precision the position of these invaders:

> The Princess and her little retinue represent the first penetration
> of the park by the normal world beyond, a world composed of
> different and colder elements than the fairy-tale environment
> within. Through them, in some sense, the voice of Reality
> speaks, and although they seem to fit perfectly into the landscape
> of the park, indulge in highly formal, elaborate skirmishes of wit
> with each other and with the men, they are somehow detached
> from this world of illusion and artificiality in a way that none of
> its original inhabitants are. The contrived and fashionable poses
> which they adopt are in a sense less serious, more playful than
> those of the other characters, and they are conscious all the time,
> as even Berowne is not, that these attitudes are merely poses, and
> Reality is something quite different. With them into the park
> they bring past time and a disturbing reminder of the world out-
> side, and from them come the first objective criticisms which pass
> beyond the scheme of the Academe to attack the men who have
> formed it. . . . In the wit of the ladies themselves, it is a certain
> edge of reality, an uncompromising logic, which cuts through
> the pleasant webs of artifice, the courtly jests and elaborations in
> the humor of the men, and emerges victorious with an unfailing
> regularity.[1]

The arrival of Marcade with the news of the French
king's death is both a supreme dramatic stroke and has

[1] Op. cit., p. 415.

unexpected results. As a dramatic stroke it clearly twins the sudden appearance of the Abbess at the height of the farcical action in the *Comedy of Errors*; and in both plays the appearance of the tall figure in black among the motley of the other persons must as sheer spectacle have been thrilling. But the Abbess introduces no new element, she merely clears up an action whose end was not in doubt. Marcade causes a double reversal and enlightenment. The play had opened with the King of Navarre toying with the idea of cheating death through achieving fame:

> Let fame, that all hunt after in their lives,
> Live regist'red upon our brazen tombs,
> And then grace us in the disgrace of death;
>
> (I, i, 1)

The reference to death was quite hollow, for real death was the last thing that Navarre had in his mind; and in the body of the play he and his fellows live in the moment, as regardless of the future as any young men have ever been. The irruption of real and present death into their mood of greatest frivolity shakes them to their depths; they will not be the same men after it. But the process does not end here. It is because they are truly shaken that they can make the women see, as they had not done before, that for all their frivolous behaviour their professed love was not altogether affected; it had some core of truth. And so for the chief characters the world begins to assume a touch of its true colours, and the women are able to dictate the terms under which they will accept their lovers in the setting of true social life.

vi. THE END

The contention, made at the end of my second section, that Shakespeare left the issue of his action in doubt goes so much against normal opinion that I ought to add something concerning it. The nearest approach to scepticism I have encountered is from Quiller-Couch in his introduction to the *New Cambridge Shakespeare* edition: 'Love's labour has been lost for a while, since mourning in this world often interrupts it, perhaps for its good: but it shall be redeemed anon, we hope'.[1] Such a hope may be legitimate but only if it is balanced by the opposing doubt whether the young men have been shaken and matured enough by the intrusion of death on their world of fantasy to enable them to go through with their penances: is there anything in their past behaviour to justify Quiller-Couch's tentative optimism? Other critics have no qualms about the happy ending. Miss Roesen writes of the young man who has been given the harshest penance and who thus is the least likely to make good:

> At the end of the year, love's labors will be won for Berowne, and he will receive Rosaline's love, not in the half real world of the park, but in the actuality outside its walls. Thus the play which began with a paradox, that of the Academe, closes with one as well. Only through the acceptance of the reality of Death are life and love in their fullest sense made possible for the people of the play.[2]

While believing the last sentence to be true, I yet persist in asking: does the play really make it plain that the young men will seize the possibility referred to? Again, John Vyvyan is quite assured of a happy ending:

> Love's labour is lost in this play because it is a labour of affectation not sincerity. But it will be won—so we are promised at the end—by service and sacrifice.[3]

[1] xiii. [2] Op. cit., p. 425.
[3] Op. cit., p. 54.

I fail to see any sign of such a promise in Shakespeare's
text: all we know is that it *could* be won.[1]

But I go further than saying that such certainties are
not borne out by the text; I would say that they violate
the play's whole complexion. The main substance of the
play is of uncertainties and irregularities. The principal
men are in the muddy state of adolescence; the principal
women, placed in a queer position anyhow, in a kind of
campers' or caravan existence, and puzzled by the antics
of the men, assume the poses that seem to befit their
position and which are not the natural ones of their own
choosing. Most of the other characters are freaks, uncertain either of themselves or of the larger world without.
It is true that into this world breaks the sobering fact of
death but it does not work its complete sobering effect
while the play's true action lasts, for the two principal
penances imposed are macabre and in their ways as remote from the larger world as have been the actions of
those who have to undergo them. They are also perfectly
fitted to expiate those actions. In fact they look back into
the body of the play more than they look forward to the
new life which may or may not emerge. It is perfectly apt
that Navarre, promoter of the bogus academy, should
have to endure the hardships he had planned in theory.
But the setting of those hardships, the 'forlorn and naked
hermitage,/Remote from all the pleasures of the world'
(V, ii, 783), where its occupant will be subject to 'frost
and fasts, hard lodging and thin weeds', is strangely grim

---

[1] Walter Oakeshott in his book on Raleigh, *The Queen and the Poet*
(London, 1960), p. 109, thinks that it is not the four men of Navarre
whose labour of love is lost, for they will achieve matrimony, but Armado.
Armado is Raleigh, and his labour of love is the verse he addressed in vain
to his royal mistress.

and remote from the clear light of the common Elizabethan day. As for Berowne,

> You shall this twelvemonth term from day to day
> Visit the speechless sick, and still converse
> With groaning wretches; and your task shall be,
> With all the fierce endeavour of your wit,
> To enforce the pained impotent to smile.
>
> (V, ii, 838)

It is an apt penance, for, as Rosaline goes on to explain, the success of Berowne's notorious sallies of satire depended on the applause of fools easily provoked to laughter. Let him now try his luck with another kind of audience. But it is a grotesque and macabre penance, remote from the norm of ordinary life; and Berowne protests against it in horror:

> To move wild laughter in the throat of death?
> It cannot be; it is impossible;
> Mirth cannot move a soul in agony.
>
> (V, ii, 843)

And of course it points backward: in its substance to his wild laughter when the actors are being baited and Armado and Costard hooted on to their duel, and in its grotesqueness to the other, if different, grotesquenesses of the past action of the play. To demand clarity just here, to impose on this lovely medley of uncertainties the cut-and-driedness of a happy ending is to offend against the whole spirit of the play; whereas to leave the issue in doubt makes us continue to dwell on all the things that have charmed us before.

Of course full reality does break in; but not through the action of the play. It is the songs of the cuckoo and the owl, about spring and winter, that tell of real life, of a life accepted and enjoyed in spite of its knowledge of death and of the dying in their hospitals, and which release a surprise on us as thrilling as when Mercade interrupted the wild hubbub in the park of Navarre. Miss Roesen[1] would have it that the songs are not contrasted with the substance of the play but echo different parts of it. Thus the embroidery-like picture of the enamelling of flowers echoes the artificial picture of the park of Navarre. But the flowers enumerated—daisies, violets, cuckoo-flowers, and buttercups—are none of them exotic; and I cannot see that in enumerating them Shakespeare meant to evoke anything more remote than an English spring when the weather is fine. It may be legitimate to picture a tapestry background to the Cloudcuckooland that is the park of Navarre, but it certainly did not breed ordinary daisies and buttercups, any more than it was concerned with housekeeping or eating. I wrote of the urban solidity of Ephesus in the *Comedy of Errors* and of dinner being a matter of importance there; but the dinner that Holofernes enjoyed at the house of one of his pupils was not a real dinner but a forum for his eloquence. Nor is the deer that the princess shot a real beast, though it has its function in provoking fantastic thoughts, snobbery, and bad puns from the actors. But the larks and the turtles of the spring song are real birds, while greasy Joan keeling her pot in winter is an emblem of real housekeeping. And I find no reason for withdrawing the words that I wrote in another context:

> When, after the fantastic medley of courtly affectations, Shakespeare suddenly shows us his maidens bleaching their summer frocks and Tom bearing logs into the hall, we make no reservations but merely think: that is life; then, and now.[2]

[1] Op. cit., p. 411.   [2] *Shakespeare's History Plays*, p. 146.

What are we to make of the few words of prose that follow the songs? In the traditional texts they run as follows:

Arm. The words of Mercury are harsh after the songs of Apollo. You that way: we this way.

(V, ii, 917)

Unfortunately, in the First Quarto, the prime authority for the text, the last sentence is missing and the first sentence is printed in larger type and not attributed to any speaker. It is the First Folio that prints both sentences and attributes them to Armado, or rather to *Brag.* after its common habit. If we rely solely on the Quarto, we cannot but conclude that the single sentence looks like an extrinsic aphorism, added by an unknown hand to the body of the text, and that the play ended with the songs. If we can trust the Folio, we are given an exquisitely appropriate ending. The last six words proclaim division; suggest uncertainty. They take us back to the play itself and, a miracle of economy, hint that we must leave things hanging.

Chapter VII

THE MERCHANT OF VENICE

i. PRESUPPOSITIONS: ADVISABLE AND INADVISABLE

THERE is a discrepancy between what the public and what the critics have made of the *Merchant of Venice*. The public have loved it and found little wrong with it; the critics have given conflicting interpretations or have found much wrong with it. W. P. Ker even went so far as to accuse it of fundamental disharmony.

> A story like that of the *Three Caskets* or the *Pound of Flesh* is perfectly consistent with itself in its original popular form. It is inconsistent with the form of elaborate drama, and with the lives of people who have souls of their own, like Portia or Shylock. Hence in the drama which uses the popular story as its ground-plan, the story is never entirely reduced into conformity with the spirit of the chief characters. The caskets and the pound of flesh, in despite of all the author's pains with them, are imperfectly harmonised; the primitive and barbarous imagination in them retains an inconvenient power of asserting its discordance with the principal parts of the drama.[1]

In this dispute I am on the side of the public, thinking some of the critics' interpretations far-fetched and Ker's condemnation the exact opposite of the truth. Not that Shakespeare's task was not even more complex than Ker indicated, for it went beyond that of humanizing fairy-tales and included one of the formulas of classico-Italian comedy: that of the young folk getting the better of a

---

[1] *Epic and Romance* (London, 1922), p. 36.

182

harsh and avaricious father by trickery. As Grumio said in the *Taming of the Shrew*, 'Here's no knavery! See, to beguile the old folks, how the young folks lay their heads together' (*Taming of the Shrew*, I, ii, 135). The episode of the rings, too, is comic not romantic. Thus, Shakespeare was committed to making his play a comedy as well as a fairy romance. Allowing for a couple of queer lapses and a certain predisposition in his audience not shared by ourselves, the play triumphs and, within its well-defined limits, emerges a masterpiece.

The two lapses need not detain us long. The first, indeed, looks like a cut, not an error of judgement. It has to do with Bassanio's speech when he chooses the right casket. In the two corresponding scenes both Morocco and Arragon, in speeches of fifty-five and forty-eight lines respectively, pondered the inscriptions on the caskets; Bassanio, on the other hand, speaks only thirty-three lines and says nothing about the inscriptions. Now this lets us down, for in a fairy-tale we feel cheated if we do not get a strict pattern. If Morocco and Arragon pondered on the inscriptions, Bassanio was bound by the rules of faery to do the same. Moreover, the inscription on the casket he chooses—'Who chooseth me must give and hazard all he hath'—is so perfectly apt to Bassanio himself and to the whole tenor of the play that it is criminal to omit a reference to it at this of all places. The other lapse is the way in which Portia describes how she and Nerissa will disguise themselves as youths. It occurs (III, iv) immediately after she has sent Balthazar to Doctor Bellario: that is when she has the serious matter of Antonio's rescue principally in mind and when she is determined to personate a Doctor of Laws. Nothing here could be more inept than the boast of 'proving the prettier fellow of the

two' and speaking 'between the change of man and boy/
With a reed-voice.' Possibly Shakespeare wished by his
tone here to make it perfectly clear before the trial scene
that the play was a comedy and that we need have no
anxiety about the issue of the trial; but, if so, he made it
clear at a cost.

As to the predisposition in an audience, we recognize
pretty well by now that in Shakespeare we must be ready
for a character to cease being his differentiated self,
spout a piece of impersonal rhetoric, and revert to that
self. There is no need now to justify Enobarbus's poetical
rhetoric in picturing Cleopatra on Cydnus by psychological
standards: 'Shakespeare deliberately put the poetry into
the mouth of a hard-bitten, unpoetical soldier to enhance
the power of Cleopatra's beauty; so great was it that in
spite of himself he was moved to poetry.' We are content
to accept Enobarbus at that moment as an actor reciting
a piece of rhetoric necessary to the context. But in the
Merchant of Venice we must be content with more: with
seeing a character turning into a different character or
into an allegory. We must, in fact, read the play as we
have to read Spenser: with no fixed expectations of what a
character is like or will turn into. The Portia who begins
as a witty young woman turns into the princess of the
Beautiful Mountain, dangerous and difficult of access,
into the perfectly dutiful and affectionate wife, into a
tomboy, into an allegory of Mercy, and ends as something
not unlike her first self, only maturer and more in command of every situation. Bassanio, beginning as the good-
hearted but improvident young man of conventional
comedy, gathers dignity and poise to qualify as the fairy
prince subjected to his ordeal. And I think there would
have been less trouble over Shylock if critics had been

less anxious to make him quite self-consistent. Bred on Spenser and other allegory, an Elizabethan audience would have had no difficulty in accepting these transformations; while it is worth recollecting that in *Richard III* Shakespeare had recently created a character who changed from a credible, if eccentric, human being into the monstrous villain of melodrama. Or consider the first scene of that popular play, Dekker's *Old Fortunatus*.[1] Fortunatus begins as a humorous beggar, speaking in prose. He then sleeps and has a vision in which Fortune offers him the choice of 'Wisdom, strength, health, beautie, long life, and riches' (*Old Fortunatus*, I, i, 211). In reply he addresses Fortune and the fates in verse of this kind:

> Give me but leave to borrow wonder's eye,
> To look (amaz'd) at thy bright majestie . . .
>
> (I, i, 214)

> Daughters of Jove and the unblemisht night,
> Most righteous Parce, guide my Genius right.
>
> (I, i, 222)

And his speech before he makes his choice is as poetical and as educated as anything Portia's suitors say before choosing between the caskets. On waking, Fortunatus reverts to his old self. As to Spenser, consider the anonymous *Grim the Collier of Croydon*, clearly composed for a popular audience. The introductory scene is in Hades, with the judges sitting on the case of Spenser's Malbecco. They wonder whether women are in fact as bad as Malbecco makes them out to be and send Belphegor in human shape to live on earth for a year and then come

[1] In Dekker, *Dramatic works*, ed. F. Bowers, vol. I, 1953.

back and report. On the report Malbecco will be judged. There are two points of interest for us here: first, the assumption that a mixed theatre audience will be familiar with Spenser, and second, the character of Malbecco. Of all Spenser's characters Malbecco shows the widest transformation: from realistic jealous old man to an allegorical figure of Jealousy. Familiar with Spenser's Malbecco, an Elizabethan audience would have no difficulty in accepting the many changes of Portia. Actually, modern audiences have managed pretty well to exercise the kind of adaptability I have been postulating and have insisted on adoring the *Merchant of Venice* as a perfectly viable stage-play.

One thing that has prevented men from accepting the *Merchant* unequivocally as a masterpiece is the ease of execution. Can anything so pellucid in sense and of so smooth a gliding have really called forth the author's full powers? In retort, I would point to a remark of Balzac in *La Cousine Bette*. The author is reflecting on the sense of ease in some of Raphael's paintings and of strain in others, and he goes on:

> In the begetting of works of art there is as much chance in the character of the offspring as there is in a family of children; that some will be happily graced, born beautiful, and costing their mother little suffering, creatures on whom everything smiles and with whom everything succeeds.

The *Merchant* is like one of these fortunate children. Or consider this common experience in learning to speak a foreign language. There are times when all goes wrong, when the knowledge you think you command simply refuses to make itself available and you stutter as you may not have done a week ago; and there are times when all goes right, when all your resources await your pleasure and you find yourself a better linguist than you ever thought you could be. Some such happy facility appears to mark the *Merchant of Venice*, whatever in actual fact were the pains that it cost its maker. To have achieved this happy facility in compassing a varied, even apparently incongruous, array of themes was one of Shakespeare's major triumphs; and I rejoice to be able to quote Granville-Barker to the effect that the play 'is—for what it is —as smoothly and completely successful, its means being as well fitted to its end, as anything Shakespeare wrote'.[1]

I have accused the critics of advancing far-fetched interpretations and would like to point one out, pleading at the same time for a renewed simplicity of vision and a renewed heed to what the text tells us. As long as I can remember and until very recently, I have taken it for granted that the young men encompassing Antonio were a light-hearted and prodigal set; in fact the sort of young men you would expect in Venice on the evidence of the *Toccata of Galuppi*. I cannot say whence I derived that impression; but this very ignorance suggests its prevalence, its being generally taken for granted. Quiller-Couch gives the doctrine in its extreme form in his introduction to the *New Cambridge Shakespeare* edition, where he called Antonio not only the careful merchant but

> the indolent patron of a circle of wasters, 'born to consume the fruits of this world', heartless, or at least unheedful, while his life lies in jeopardy through his tender, extravagantly romantic friendship for one of them.

Turn to the text, and you find the very opposite of heedlessness among Antonio's friends. In II, viii, after Salerio

[1] *Prefaces to Shakespeare*, second series (1930), p. 68.

has described the parting of Bassanio from Antonio, Solanio says

> I pray thee, let us go and find him out,
> And quicken his embraced heaviness
> With some delight or other.

(II, viii, 51)

And when in III, iii, Shylock meets Antonio before the trial seeking exercise outside the prison in charge of the gaoler, Solanio is there to keep Antonio company. In the first scene Antonio's friends are sincerely worried about his state of mind, though they may seem to joke about it. Even the irrepressible Gratiano, the buffoon of the circle, is sincere and well-intentioned in his remonstrance with Antonio (as he says, 'I love thee, and 'tis my love that speaks' (I, i, 87)) even if he is far from understanding his trouble. He seriously warns Antonio not to be melancholy for the sake of 'opinion', which means here 'reputation' or even 'publicity'. Once, in real life, a more distinguished buffoon than Gratiano, Bernard Shaw, said of a more distinguished neurotic than Antonio, T. E. Lawrence: 'he takes cover in the lime-light'. Gratiano's speech is, in essence, a warning against such behaviour and a hint that the sufferer had better pull himself together. He is in fact the well-meaning eupeptic who cannot believe in the plight of those less happily extroverted than himself. Lorenzo in his honeymoon excitement makes free with the money his Jessica has lifted from her father but, arrived in Belmont, he shows the most impeccable approval of Portia's generosity in allowing Bassanio to hurry to Venice on Antonio's account and pays this tribute to Antonio's high worth:

> But if you knew to whom you show this honour,
> How true a gentleman you send relief,

How dear a lover of my lord your husband,
I know you would be prouder of the work
Than customary bounty can enforce you.

(III, iv, 5)

In fact Antonio's friends are a perfectly decent lot, of the kind you might find in the Inns of Court in Shakespeare's London, gay but not vicious and with at least an underlying sense of responsibility. That is, if you do not sentimentalize Shylock and damn the whole pack of them in disgust at Gratiano's jeers at him when he sees his game has been lost.

ii. SHYLOCK

In some ways there is little need to speak of Shylock, for present opinion, represented for instance by the editors of the new Arden and Players' editions of the *Merchant*, has settled into a satisfactory position between the tough and the tender interpreters. But something I must say, for I conjecture that the blackening of Antonio's friends depends ultimately on a false conception of Shylock.

Shakespeare's Shylock has been the victim of the great actor. No other male character in the *Merchant* offered sufficient scope for him. All you can do with Bassanio is to make him, the male charmer, as manly and as charming as possible; there are no lateral possibilities. And mere male charm does not suffice the great actor. Antonio lacks emphasis and is too passive and withdrawn to meet the requirements. It would indeed be possible to specialize him into the tortured homosexual and extract a bit of sensationalism in that way; but that would not have suited the taste of the last two centuries, when the big actor's Shylock was being created. These exhaust the list of the

189

other potentially major male parts, and Shylock remained the one possible victim of fruitful distortion. By exaggerating certain lines where we are invited to see Shylock's point of view and playing down or forgetting others that balance the impression made by these it was possible to fabricate a Shylock who was more sinned against than sinning, an intruder from the realm of tragedy, and thus a man of a dimension nobler than that of any other male character: in sum, a character worth the attention of the great actor.

This weighting of Shylock was bound to have consequences beyond itself. In the measure in which you increase your sympathy with him in the same measure you turn against those who rejoice or gloat over his downfall. Antonio's companions cease to be decent young men and become callous wasters. Then, any upsetting of the balance causes an unduly violent reaction. Thus, those who have seen that Shakespeare's text simply will not admit of the great actor's Shylock, for instance E. E. Stoll[1] and René Pruvost,[2] have, in reaction, made just a little too much of Shylock's undoubted affinity to the conventional types of usurer, Puritan, and Pantaloon familiar to an Elizabethan audience, as if Shakespeare was not capable of having it both ways: that is of satisfying conventional expectations up to a point and yet preserving his freedom to extend his sympathies beyond anything his audience could have glimpsed and to make the conventional issue into the unique. They thus do an injustice to Shakespeare as surely as do those who hold that Shylock ran away with him during composition and forced his maker to enlarge the stature for which he was first designed.

[1] E.g., in 'Shakespeare's Jew', in *University of Toronto Quarterly*, January, 1939, pp. 139–54.
[2] *Les Langues Modernes*, 1951, pp. 99–109.

It cannot be too strongly asserted that Shylock, unin-
flated and unsentimentalized, remains one of Shakespeare's most wonderful creations and that he perfectly
suits and promotes the romantic comedy in which he
occurs. The 'tough' critics are correct in holding that Shylock was malevolent from the beginning and is never
anything else; but in the scene where he first appears, and
which should dictate our feelings about him, the strongest
impression he gives, one that Shakespeare creates immediately with an incredible economy of words, is of
strangeness. Shylock is utterly and irretrievably the alien.
His slowness of speech, with its repetitions of what Bassanio has already said—'Three thousand ducats, for three
months, and Antonio bound', etc.—betokens not only a
man temperamentally repugnant to the lively Venetians
but a whole alien code of manners. The Venetians can be
formal enough on occasions, but Bassanio is far too con-
temptuous of the processes of finance to be willing to be-
stow the gift of his formality on *them*. On the other hand
they are a big portion of Shylock's restricted existence, and
he loves to draw them out and to savour them. That love,
alien to the Venetians, is yet a conceivable human feeling;
and Shakespeare, who was interested in all such human
feelings, puts himself in Shylock's place and puts words
into Shylock's mouth expressive of that love. In so doing
he may be said to sympathize with Shylock, but only in a
restricted sense of the word. In no sense does he take sides
with him. When, in actual life, we encounter abruptly
alien habits of mind we experience revulsion in the first
place, but on it curiosity may quickly follow. The Venetians in encountering Shylock never got beyond revulsion;
and Shakespeare was being true enough to life in thus res-
tricting them. But he was free also to express his own

curiosity and larger vision by causing Shylock to present here and elsewhere his own strange world. He does not expect us to like the picture. Shylock's house was a hell of gloom, puritanical and museless; and his Jessica is justified in leaving it in favour of light and the prospects of a Christian heaven. But in the background there is the synagogue and the antique world of the Old Testament; and I think we are justified in thinking that Shylock's reference to his wife and her ring is meant to denote a kind of ordered domestic life in past days. And as to his daughter, at least he was vulnerably dependent on her and perhaps loved her in his harsh way. Again, there is 'sympathy', but of the restricted kind.

What may not have been noted about Shylock is his spiritual stupidity. If the Venetians take no stock of Shylock's world, neither does he of theirs; and with less excuse. It is an unpleasant fact of life that a dominant class is less apt to study the dispositions of its subordinates than the other way round. It is also common sense, if you are a subordinate, to recognize the fact and to fall in with your fellows. Hence my assertion that Shylock had less excuse. He is quite self-absorbed and incapable of watching others. Shakespeare brings this out wonderfully in his great speeches (III, i) to Salario and Solanio about Antonio's scorn and *all* of his hostile acts to racial prejudice. It never begins to enter his head that Antonio may have genuine scruples about usury and that his acts in redeeming the debts of imprisoned Christians may have been motivated by disinterested kindness. And Shylock's stupidity becomes all the more convincing dramatically, when, in his lashings out, he strikes in the Christians the very sin he has been in the act of exemplifying. 'If a Jew wrong a Christian, what is his humility? Revenge.' I say the same

sin as Shylock's, for the Venetians, in excluding the Jew
from the scope of their Christian code of conduct, were
indeed being stupid, were denying to a portion of the
human race something which of its very essence applied,
if to any, to all. Again, it is a mistake to think that Shakespeare was here so carried away by his Shylock that he took
sides with him against his enemies. If it is necessary to
define Shakespeare's position, it is this: the Venetians are
better than the Jew, but they do not always act on that
betterness; the Jew is worse, but not without excuse for
being so. But, of course, Shakespeare does not take sides:
he presents things as he sees them, to the enlargement of
our sympathies if we are content to follow him. One more
example of Shylock's stupidity is his mentioning his
daughter and his ducats in the same breath. He has not
the sense to see that others may find here an incongruity.
Shakespeare is not any the less understanding of Shylock
for having made him stupid. He created him as he created
another character, stupid in her own way, Mrs Quickly;
and no one would dream of saying that he failed in sympathy here. He also had a good reason for making his
Shylock stupid. Experience has shown that in the trial
scene producers and readers have sought to enlarge Shylock into a figure of tragic dimensions, to the detriment of
the whole shape of the play. Tragic is precisely what
Shylock should not be; and Shakespeare made his Shylock
stupid, as Conrad in the *Secret Agent* made Winnie Ver-
lock stupid, in order to preserve the comic predominance
of his composition. Stupid people can be pathetic, but
tragic never. Shylock's culminating stupidity occurs in
the trial scene; and I have written at length about it in my
Essays Literary and Educational (1962). There I maintain
that Portia, in her role as Mercy, knowing she has her

infallible charm for saving Antonio's life, spends her eloquence in trying to make Shylock save his own soul, an attempt which he cannot even begin to recognize.

I can now revert to the first point I made in talking of Shylock: the strangeness of his Jewish world. It is because of that strangeness that we can move to the other strange world of Belmont and the romantic improbabilities of the casket theme, without inconvenience. Many elements went to the composition of Shylock, as they did to that of Falstaff; but, situated at Belmont, we can, on account of that strangeness, see him not as the pantaloon of comedy, or as the joyless Puritan, but as the hero's enemy in the fairy-tale, the simple embodiment of the powers of evil.

iii. BASSANIO AND ANTONIO

I conjecture that there is still some uneasiness about Bassanio and his fitness to be Portia's lover. Orlando was unfortunate and wrestled well; and we accept Rosalind's passion without trouble. But Bassanio is active in nothing but in borrowing money. By modern standards Portia's infatuation was unmotivated. True, in the caskets scene Bassanio speaks nobly and, if you follow the logic of the poetry, was well worthy to be Portia's suitor. But you cannot invoke the logic of the poetry to ennoble Bassanio when in the first scene he confesses to Antonio that he has been extravagant and has run badly into debt:

> 'Tis not unknown to you, Antonio,
> How much I have disabled mine estate
> By something showing a more swelling port
> Than my faint means would grant continuance;
>
> (I, i, 122)

It would be possible here to think of Bassanio as the ordinary young man of classical comedy: a good sort, heart in the right place and all that, but extravagant and not yet settled down. His windy rhetoric describing his debts would be the comic expression of his embarrassment at having to ask Antonio for still further advances of money. But, if we take this line, we do so less by instinct than by arguing ourselves into it. And I rather think that here is one of the cases where we have to reflect on contemporary conditions in order to understand and justify it. From the moment of his entry it would have been plain to an Elizabethan audience that Bassanio, both by his bearing and from his clothes, was the dazzling male charmer, the young man so handsome as to be irresistible to any heiress, the inevitable inspirer of female devotion.[1] We are meant to feel in the same way about Bertram in *All's Well*. He was 'unbaked and doughy', a lout, and in character unworthy of his Helena. But he was devilishly handsome, a man with whom *ex hypothesi* she could be desperately in love; and an Elizabethan spectator would have had no need to be sceptical and ask awkward questions about psychological probabilities. One must also remember that though the Elizabethans in their poetry had much to say about female beauty they still retained much primitive convention in the matter of marriage. Now, by primitive convention it is the courting man's duty to be handsome and the courted woman's to be rich. The convention survived in the form in which the Greek newspapers used to put the announcements of engagements to be married. These stated that the very beautiful youth, Mr X, intends

[1] In the 1637 Quarto, where the names of the characters are first listed, he is called 'an Italian lord', while Antonio is a merchant and his other friends 'gentlemen of Venice and companions with Bassanio'. Here, therefore, Bassanio is made to stand out.

to wed the very richly dowered girl, Miss Y. It is in such a context that one must think of the jibes in *Henry VI* about the poverty of his queen or these lines in a speech by Owen Tudor when courting Katherine of France, widow of Henry V, in Warner's *Albion's England*. Owen boasts of his pedigree, which of course was important, and then hints at his physical qualifications that will match what he cannot supply and what she can and should, wealth:

If gentry, madam, might convey so great a good to me,
From ancient King Cadwallader I have my pedigree.
If wealth be said my want, I say your Grace doth want no wealth,
And my supplyment shall be love, employed to your health.

(Chap. 29, Bk. 6)

And, generally, readers should recollect, what most of them know very well, the importance of the dowry in medieval and Elizabethan times. In brief, we must get over our difficulty with Bassanio through the thought that for Shakespeare's contemporaries it did not exist.

There should thus be little difficulty in siting Bassanio correctly in the play. With his friend, Antonio, it is otherwise. The melancholy of the title-character, with which the play begins, has mostly been evaded or played down; and critics have been unwilling to face the unacceptable truth that either the melancholy, made so prominent by its position, contributes something vital to the play, or that Shakespeare committed a major artistic error by arousing expectations he never fulfilled. It is vain, for instance, to say that the Elizabethans thought melancholy foreboded a misfortune and that Antonio's melancholy is introduced at the beginning to indicate that trouble awaits him. Not only is Antonio's melancholy too deep-seated and too long insisted on for it to mean no more than that, but Antonio's

196

melancholy is matched by Portia's when she first appears, and Portia was anything but unfortunate. When, far after the time has passed for forebodings, Antonio calls himself the 'tainted wether of the flock' it is sheer evasion to apply to his melancholy any trivial explanation. A recent attempt, therefore, to give it due weight is greatly to be welcomed.

The attempt I refer to is found in an essay by Graham Midgley on the *Merchant*. Midgley is agreeably forthright and would persuade us to take the play in a very novel manner. He seeks to take the emphasis off the love-story and put it on the contrasted lonelinesses of Shylock and Antonio. This is how he states his main thesis:

> The two focal points of the play are Shylock and, not the lovers of the romance theme, but Antonio, and that the world of love and marriage is not opposed by Shylock, but rather paralleled by Venetian society as a whole, social, political, and economic. The scheme of the play is, if I may reduce it to ratio terms: As Shylock is to Venetian society, so is Antonio to the world of love and marriage. The relationship of these two to these two worlds is the same, the relationship of an outsider. The play is, in effect, a twin study in loneliness. The fact that these two outcasts, these two lonely men, only meet in the cruel circumstances they do, adds an irony and pathos to the play which lift it out of the category of fairy tale or romance.[1]

With many of Midgley's contentions I disagree. First, I do not think the loneliness of the two principal men to be the main theme. On the contrary, the play is a romantic comedy; and Shakespeare takes every care to see that it is so. Thus, for instance, Portia gives Bassanio her ring at the very first chance after he has made the right choice, and well before the messenger comes from Venice with the

[1] *Essays in Criticism*, April 1960, p. 121.

bad news about Antonio. The episode of the ring, purely comic, is an organic part of Shakespeare's main source, *Il Pecorone*, and he took it over as such, making the fifth act no mere afterthought but crucial to the whole play; and the trend of that act is either romantic or comic, and only in a most minor way anything else. Midgley also revives the notion of a much injured Shylock, talking of his 'proud and patient bearing' and of his being 'sober rather than miserly in his domestic life'. And at the same time he takes his picture of the Venetian youth from Browning rather than Shakespeare. Venetian society is

> a world of golden youth, richly dressed, accustomed to luxury, to feasting, to masking, of a comparatively easy virtue and of a religious outlook which, though orthodox, hardly strikes one as deep.

And in his anxiety to match Act IV, which presents the unhappy ruin of Shylock, with Act V, which he maintains has the unhappy ruin of Antonio as its master theme, he strains the evidence far beyond what it will bear. He finds Antonio's welcome to Belmont hollow and that the happy couples forget all about him at the end. He is alone. He insists that the end is that of the *Yeoman of the Guard*, where the lonely man stays behind, quite neglected by all his fellows. There is not the least evidence for this; and I should be surprised if, in the performances Shakespeare contrived after his own liking, Portia did not have the courtesy to make him enter the house along with Bassanio and herself.[1]

---

[1] Granville-Barker pictures the end thus: 'The play ends, pleasantly and with formality, as a fairy-tale should . . . Portia and Bassanio, Antonio . . . must pace off the stage in their stately Venetian way, while Gratiano's harmless ribaldry is tossed to the audience as an epilogue.' (Op. cit., p. 107.)

Nevertheless, Midgley has made an important point in insisting on the loneliness of the two principal men; and his analysis of Antonio's loneliness is borne out by the text and adds something both new and true to the meaning of the play. It has of course been noted already that there is much in common between the first section of the sonnets and the sentiments expressed by Antonio for Bassanio. But no one so far has given those sentiments their proper weight. Antonio suffers from a self-abnegating passion that quenches the springs of vitality in him and makes him the self-chosen outcast from society: the 'tainted wether of the flock' (IV, i, 114). Annotators seem to have passed over *wether* as if it were a synonym for *ram* or even a mere variation of *sheep*. But I cannot believe that Shakespeare did not mean us to accept and give weight to its full significance. Antonio now sees himself as useless. Before Bassanio left him for Portia, his life had some direction; now it has none. And he can only watch from without the crowd of those who are sure of their directions. I do not think Antonio a study of homosexuality; but Shakespeare presented him as essentially a lonely figure, strikingly different from all the sociable folk he has to do with, except Shylock.

Such a presentation enriches the play and makes sense of a character in it who had hitherto been meaningless. Nevertheless, the theme, enriching as it is, remains subordinate. It is absolutely characteristic of Shakespeare to be critical of the very things which he seems to mind most about. Antonio and Shylock, going clean counter to the things the play seems most to stand for, provide the admirable assurance that the picture of life here shown and apparently calculated to absorb all our attention is yet incomplete, that Shakespeare in creating a complex but

coherent and satisfying world yet refuses to be satisfied.
Taking all truth as his province, he must never allow a
single side of it, however absorbing or lovely or terrible,
to pass unrelated, to be cut off from the totality that lies
outside.

IV. THE TOTAL EFFECT

Granville-Barker, like W. W. Lawrence and Middleton
Murry[1] (who derives from Lawrence without directly saying so) makes the fairy-tale substance of the *Merchant of
Venice* the centre of the meaning. Shakespeare had chosen
two traditional, utterly familiar stories, and his

> practical business was simply so to charge them with humanity
> that they did not betray belief in the human beings presenting
> them, yet not so uncompromisingly that the stories themselves
> become ridiculous.[2]

This is true as far as it goes but it also puts things too
simply. Shakespeare's main source, *Il Pecorone*, is not a
pure fairy-tale, for it includes the comic theme of the lost
ring. Nor does he keep the Shylock story uncontaminated,
for he includes in it the current comic motive, classico-
Italian in origin, of a child for the sake of love deceiving
a harsh and miserly parent and the Morality theme of
Justice against Mercy. Shakespeare's business was to extract from all ingredients, romantic, comic, and Morality,
the greatest possible meaning.

Whatever the complexity or even seeming incongruity
of the matter of the *Merchant of Venice*, its effect is one of
harmony and serenity. The cause is the run of the verse
and prose, which is easy, unimpeded, reassuring. The

spirit that animates the rhetoric is that of sheer goodwill. That spirit animates the *Midsummer Night's Dream* also, but with such great differences that we never suspect the least tautology. The *Dream* ranges over a larger section of the cosmos and is seen from a greater distance. The *Merchant*, though a fairy tale, is occupied with a smaller part of society and is seen from near at hand. In the *Dream* the narrative counts for little, and we have rather a series of juxtaposed human relations. In the *Merchant*, the narrative counts for much and with it the romance or fairy-tale substance. In fact, the *Merchant* is the play of Shakespeare where the mental feelings proper to the romance, as I have described them in my introductory chapter, figure largest. There are three tasks or ordeals to be performed or endured. Bassanio must survive the ordeal of the caskets; Portia must achieve the rescue of Antonio; Antonio must endure and survive imprisonment and danger to his life. Possibly Lorenzo and Jessica provide a fourth example. Once the ordeals have been survived, happiness, of indefinite duration, ensues; except for Antonio, who is deliberately made an exception to the general rule. I pointed out that this process, recurrent in the fairy tale, represented a universal trend of human feeling. In spite of the immense counter-attraction of luck, of the delight of getting something for nothing, mankind believes that it is better to earn your happiness and approves the rhythms of the successful voyage, not without danger, or of the man setting out to work in the morning, achieving something difficult or at least solid, and then, appropriately tired, returning home to relax. It is because Shakespeare constructed the *Merchant* on these excessively simple but universal feelings that his play has enjoyed so immense a popularity.

V. THE FIFTH ACT

Granville-Barker put the beginning of this act, that is the lyrical night-piece presented by Lorenzo and Jessica before Portia's entry, in terms of a lovely bit of time-wasting to allow Portia and Jessica to change their clothes from male disguise to female elegance. Doubtless he was right, but, if he really meant to stop there, only in a most limited sense; for this night-piece is the very thing into which the rest of the play issues. The storms are over, the ship has come to port, the bad man has been thwarted and can be forgotten; and the poet has let himself in for the terrifyingly difficult task of presenting sheer goodwill and felicity without becoming strained, pietistic, or sentimental. He succeeds by economy and never allowing his expression of these things to sever connection with the critical spirit. The lyrical beauty of the 'In such a night' opening is so powerful that we may miss what Shakespeare has done to keep it wholesome. In itself it expresses the desire of man in his innocent mood for an earthly paradise. Yet with what cunning Shakespeare keeps this strong and so easily corrupted desire within bounds. For one thing he begins with a glance at Shylock and the troubles that have just been surmounted. The classical tales he presents are all sad but through the enchanting serenity of the verse he sets them at a distance; the old, unhappy things are less so than far-off. And through this distancing Shakespeare bids us do the same to the unhappy things that so recently have thrust themselves upon us. Then, for the effect it has, the full lyrical music lasts for such a short time; the thirteen and a half lines it occupies are unbelievably few compared with the depth of the impression they leave behind. And when Shakespeare turns from classical

suffering to present joy he softens his tone and drops into
banter.

> *Jessica.*   In such a night
> Did young Lorenzo swear he lov'd her well,
> Stealing her soul with many vows of faith,
> And ne'er a true one,
> *Lorenzo.*   In such a night
> Did pretty Jessica, like a little shrew,
> Slander her love, and he forgave it her.
>
> (V, i, 17)

Before reverting to the high lyrical strain Shakespeare
interposes the entries of Stephano and Launcelot with
their businesslike messages. And in Lorenzo's two
speeches on moonlight and music he glances at past un-
happiness by an oblique but, I think, certain reference to
Shylock, hater of music:

> The man that hath no music in himself,
> Nor is not mov'd with concord of sweet sounds,
> Is fit for treasons, stratagems, and spoils;
>
> (V, i, 83)

Thus the earthly paradise is never allowed to claim our
attention too long or too exclusively. Further, it has to give
way to the pure comedy of the rings, which, as far as space
goes, dominates the act. Such then were the precautions
Shakespeare took against his night-piece on goodwill and
felicity becoming pietistic and sentimental.

There was also the need to create a convincing transition from romance to comedy; and this Portia does
between her own entry and Bassanio's. It is a highly sententious passage: 'So shines a good deed in a naughty
world', 'Nothing is good, I see, without respect', and so
on; and it is a highly suggestive one. As far as I know,

little has been done to identify and follow up those suggestions; and I had better commit myself on these matters, pointing out at the same time how Shakespeare contrives his necessary transition.

Portia and Nerissa enter while the moon is still clouded over. Lorenzo had begun his speech on music in full moonshine, but during it the moon was covered, bringing the stars into greater prominence and making Lorenzo's pointing to them the more apt. When at the end of his speech he tells the musicians to 'wake Diana with a hymn' he refers to the clouds which, like bed-curtains, are drawn over the moon, a reference that is repeated[1] soon after, when Portia tells the musicians to cease playing,

> Peace, ho! the moon sleeps with Endymion,
> And would not be awak'd.
>
> (V, i, 109)

In this act there are many references to moon and daylight; and I cannot think they are arbitrary. The full moonlight with which the act begins ('The moon shines bright'), transforming the world for a brief spell into something more lovely than its usual self, corresponds to the fugitive vision of the earthly paradise the poetry conjures up. It cannot last, any more than the vision, and it must first be gently obscured and then give way to the light of common day. We must also note that Portia's entrance follows at once on Lorenzo's remarks about the evil of men who have no music in themselves; for example,

---

[1] This repetition makes Dover Wilson's interpretation (*New Cambridge Shakespeare* edition, note on p. 170) of 'wake Diana' as *keep her vigil* unlikely. J. H. Walter's interpretation (*The Players' Shakespeare* edition (London, 1960), p. 192) of the moon's sleeping with Endymion as the moon's setting is disproved by Gratiano's words to Nerissa (142) 'By yonder moon I swear you do me wrong.'

the audience cannot but add, Shylock. Coming just here, the thoughts of the audience thus directed, Portia's first words about a good deed shining in a naughty world are not mere general sententiousness but have a specific reference. Many readers, I conjecture, have taken Portia to be indulging in a piece of innocent self-satisfaction and to refer to the splendid job of work she has just brought to a happy conclusion. Or, those who think Shakespeare at one with the norm of his audience in the matter might take Portia to refer to Antonio's effort to save the soul of his enemy by forcing him to become a Christian. I doubt both these allusions. We must remember that Portia has returned to Belmont to resume her rudely interrupted bliss; her thoughts would be on Bassanio. Further, the light that reminds her of the effect of a good deed shines from her house, suggesting that the good deed in question was done there. The deed then must have been Bassanio's prompt action in giving up his present felicity to help his friend, reinforced, perhaps, by Portia's generosity in speeding him on his way. Such a reference is in harmony with what so far has been the main concern of the act: a statement of joy and goodwill after the successful surmounting of tribulations. It is a solemn statement, for I have no doubt those are right who have seen an allusion to Scripture in Portia's first three lines. But Nerissa does not continue the strain of her mistress's thought; instead, she makes it the occasion of a divagation: 'When the moon shone we did not see the candle.' Whereupon, in her next lines, Portia both continues her own thoughts about her husband and takes up Nerissa's divagation.

> So doth the greater glory dim the less:
> A substitute shines brightly as a king
> Until a king be by, and then his state

Empties itself, as doth an inland brook
Into the main of waters.

(V, i, 93)

The serene rhythm continues Portia's opening mood; and
I believe Pooler[1] is right in equating the 'substitute' with
Lorenzo and the 'king' with Bassanio. But Portia derives
her doctrine of relativity from Nerissa's observation and,
using less exalted rhythms, she develops it, making it the
means of descending from the high sentiments that have
gone before and of passing from romance to comedy. And
she is glad so to develop it, for in her final phase she is too
critical and merry a woman to allow her doting on Bassanio to spoil the little game she will play with him while
she has him so pat in her power. Therefore the crow must
be promoted to the level of the lark and the nightingale
demoted to that of the goose, presaging that even so the
husband whose good deed she has just praised so solemnly
and whom she has likened to a king must be reduced tem-
porarily to a state anything but solemn and kingly.

The crow doth sing as sweetly as the lark
When neither is attended; and I think
The nightingale, if she should sing by day
When every goose is cackling, would be thought
No better a musician than the wren.

(V, i, 102)

And with Lorenzo's entry and his recognizing Portia by
her voice, Portia sets the tone for light comedy with

He knows me as the blind man knows the cuckoo,
By the bad voice.

(V, i, 112)

Her final lines before Bassanio's entry (and which he

[1] Arden edition, London, 1905.

partly overhears) deflate the night-piece with which the act began:

> This night methinks is but the daylight sick;
> It looks a little paler; 'tis a day
> Such as the day is when the sun is hid.
>
> (V, i, 124)

Bassanio, overhearing, retorts with the magnificent compliment that if Portia, the fairy princess of Belmont, should go on ('walk') she would enlighten night as much as the sun now lights the antipodes. But she will have none of that stuff and punctures Bassanio's magnificence by a stale pun: 'Let me give light, but let me not be light' (V, i, 129). There is the most delightful, if simple and obvious irony, in the contrast between Bassanio's princely bearing on entry and the rueful state to which he is about to be reduced.

The same simple irony pervades the comedy of the rings: simple, for we now know where we are, and all we require is that the stream of the play should meander, prattling to its end. But Shakespeare gives us more than we require. For a moment he allows the bickering of his amiable characters to look serious and invokes Antonio to protect his friend from his wife's indignation; and in seeking to do so Antonio summons up into this context of light comedy all the unhappy things that for the moment have been thrust out of mind:

> I once did lend my body for his wealth,
> Which, but for him that had your husband's ring,
> Had quite miscarried: I dare be bound again,
> My soul upon the forfeit, that your lord
> Will never more break faith advisedly.
>
> (V, i, 249)

Upon such a recollection, as in music so in this drama, the action has no option but to return to its normal mood of amiable serenity and then to finish with all convenient speed.

Appendix

THE FAIRYTALE ELEMENT IN
THE TAMING OF THE SHREW

I T has long been known that the Induction and the main
plot of this play go back to folk themes. Christopher
Sly, picked up dead drunk, clothed in fine clothing, and
made to wake up in a lordly setting corresponding to his
clothes, has a long ancestry going back to the *Arabian
Nights*. Petruchio dealing with Katherina is one of a long
succession of wife-tamers. I shall have nothing to do with
the first motive except later to point to an odd instance of
its being combined with the second. But it may help us
with Shakespeare's play to distinguish between two different versions of the immemorial theme of the taming of the
shrew, the second of which has been almost ignored.

It has been usual to connect Petruchio's whirlwind wooing and his subsequent cure of his newly-wedded wife with
the crudities of the fabliau tradition; and the latest study
of Shakespeare's sources does not depart from this habit.
Geoffrey Bullough writes as follows:

> The Petruchio-Katharina story is a variant of the Shrew theme
> common in fabliaux from classical times . . . Humorous dis-
> cussions about mastery in marriage had enlivened the road to
> Canterbury in Chaucer, and the Jest Books of the Tudor age
> contained many stories of battle between the sexes . . . French
> folk-literature was peculiarly rich in stories of this nature. Their
> interest often depends on the methods adopted by the husband or
> wife to win supremacy. In a crude specimen, *Sire Hain et Dame
> Anieuse*, the husband and wife actually fight for a pair of breeches

until the husband knocks the wife into a tub of water and she has to beg for mercy. . . . Nearer to Shakespeare's theme are the tales in which the husband takes the initiative.[1]

And Bullough gives an example of the tales where the husband kills his domestic animals to show what happens to them when they are disobedient and what will happen to his bride if she offends in the same way. Among these the closest to Shakespeare is a Danish tale which not only gives this theme but includes the husband's teaching his wife to follow him in misnaming objects, and the wager on who has the most tractable wife. The story was first recounted by Svend Grundtvig and first related to the *Shrew* by Reinhold Kohler.[2] The characters are three sisters (as in *A Shrew*) who are all shrewish, and the worst of whom is tamed into a model wife as her sisters are not. It is a pity that Bullough did not include this tale in his analogues: analogues, for it can hardly rank as a source.

In all these tales it is the taming of the *wife* that is the main thing;[3] how the wife behaved before marriage is hardly touched on. But Shakespeare dwells as emphatically on the unapproachableness of the maiden as on the contrariness of the wife. It was through taking this truth into account that Peter Alexander conjectured[4] that the Petruchio–Katherina story might be 'a version on one of the great themes of literature, a comic treatment of the perilous maiden theme, where the lady is death to any

[1] Op. cit., pp. 61–2.

[2] In 'Zu Shakespeare's *The Taming of the Shrew*', in *Jahrbuch der Deutschen Shakespeare-Gesellschaft*, 1896, pp. 397–401.

[3] An exception is in a story in the Spanish *Conde Lucanor* of Don Juan Manuel, where all the men keep off the shrew, except one who is poor and wishes to better himself. See Karl Simrock, *Die Quellen des Shakespeare in Novellen Märchen und Sagen* (Bonn, 1870, second edition), I, p. 343.

[4] *Shakespeare's Life and Art* (London, 1939), p. 71.

suitor who woos her except the hero, in whose hands her apparent vices turn to virtues'. Alexander may be right, but I think Simrock takes us further when he cites the legend of *König Drosselbart* or King Thrushbeard.[1] But Simrock hardly develops his citation, on the ground that in this story the trials the shrewish wife is made to undergo duplicate those of the patient Griselda. I do not see what difference this makes, provided the resemblances with Shakespeare's play are close; and I find them close enough to wish to plead that more should be made of the story of King Thrushbeard as an analogue of the *Taming of the Shrew*.

The best-known version of the story is in the *Kinder- und Hausmärchen* of the brothers Grimm;[2] and here is a summary of it. A king had a lovely daughter but so proud that she would not look at any of her many suitors. In a last effort to get her married he organized a muster of all the eligible young men from a great distance round, lined them up according to their rank, and ordered his daughter to make her choice. With every suitor she had a fault to find and she singled out one of the kings for special rudeness, saying that his chin (which had a slight irregularity) was like a thrush's beak, whereupon her victim was nicknamed King Thrushbeard. Finally, she refused them all. Whereupon her father came to the end of his patience and swore that he would marry her to the first beggar who presented himself. A few days after, a fiddler in ragged clothes appeared at the king's palace, was admitted, and pleased the king with his music. For a reward he received the princess as his bride, and they were married then and

[1] Op. cit., pp. 351–2.
[2] For an English translation see *Grimm's Household Tales* by Margaret Hunt (London, 1884), I, pp. 203–7.

there. At once he took her to his house, a hovel with no
servants, and set her to do menial work. She did it badly
and in the end her husband procured her a place in the
kitchen of the palace of the land in which they lived. Here
she did the humblest work and used to take home the
scraps she picked up in the kitchen. One day a wedding
was to be celebrated, and as she was standing at the door
a finely dressed young man caught hold of her and
dragged her into the hall where there was to be dancing.
Here she dropped the pot in which she had hoarded some
soup and scraps, and these were scattered on the floor to
her utter confusion. As she tried to escape the fine young
man caught her, and she saw it was King Thrushbeard, who
told her that her trials were ended: that he was the fiddler
and that the wedding in course of celebration was theirs.
All her trials had been to punish her proud spirit. She duly
admitted her faults. Finally, she was clothed richly, her
father and his court joined the celebrations, and all ended
happily.

There are many versions of the story,[1] and these are
spread over a large area, including Ireland. The version
collected by the brothers Grimm differs from most of the
others in making the king force his daughter to marry;
usually the rejected prince, arriving in disguise, attracts
her by some charm, for instance an entrancing voice, or by
some tempting object, which she must have at all costs.
Often, the bride's humiliation is made worse by her husband's compelling her to steal and then seeing to it that
she is caught. But all the versions have these differences
from the wife-taming fabliau. They treat of the girl before
as well as after marriage, and she is always a princess.

[1] See J. Bolte and G. Polivka, *Anmerkungen zu den Kinder- und
Hausmärchen der Brüder Grimm* (Leipzig, 1913), I, pp. 443–9.

They do not subject her to personal violence but they cause her to be humbled, one might say educated, by a way of life the remotest possible from the one she had hitherto experienced and has finally abused. They present a sudden marriage uncelebrated at the time but celebrated with the utmost splendour after the girl has been tamed into repentance.

In Shakespeare's *Taming of the Shrew* scholars have been right in seeing traces of the fabliau treatment of the wife-taming theme. Katherina strikes Petruchio in the wooing scene, and even if he does not strike back he is coarse-mouthed to a degree. Further, the hawk-taming motive, so prominent in the scenes at Petruchio's country house, is in keeping with the violence of the fabliau treatment. Before any training was possible, a hawk's will had to be broken in a sheer head-on battle. There was no question of giving the bird a job. Nevertheless, if you take the whole play into account, its resemblances with *King Thrushbeard* are more than those with the fabliau. True, Katherina is not a princess, but her shrewishness before marriage figures largely. Her lover appears at the wedding in rags, as the fiddler did when he came to get his bride; and if in so doing he did not disguise his identity at least he disguised his inner nature. Both King Thrushbeard and Petruchio take their brides to their homes (pretended or actual) after the wedding ceremony. The tasks set the princess were educative as well as humiliating; and Petruchio, while proceeding to tame his hawk, pursues simultaneously a more kindly and educative method, trying to make Katherina see for herself the error of her ways. And lastly the wedding, uncelebrated at the time, is celebrated later in the last scene of the play, after the shrew has been tamed.

What with Chaucer and the Jest Books it is certain that Shakespeare knew the fabliau treatment of the shrewish wife. That he knew a version of the King Thrushbeard story cannot be proved; yet the resemblances between it and his play are so strong that it is likely he did. If, as is accepted, he used the Teutonic version of *Snow-white* for parts of *Cymbeline*, there is not the least improbability about his knowing the other story.

I cannot pretend that by taking this new source into account we get any help towards deciding the literary nature of the *Taming of the Shrew*. That decision remains in doubt. A Mark Van Doren finds the play quite satisfactory as a hearty farce, a Hardin Craig as a comedy where the farcical elements are remotely vestigial and need not trouble us. For myself I can neither ignore nor reconcile the two elements and am forced to conclude that the play fails in so far as it misses such a reconciliation. But however little bearing it may have on literary criticism it is an interesting possibility that in framing his play Shakespeare resorted both to fabliau and fairy-tale and that in his loyalty to both he was cheated of the unity at which surely he must have aimed.

Lastly I must point to a version of the King Thrushbeard story that includes the theme of a person waking in alien surroundings and coming to think that the past has been a dream. It comes from Corsica and was collected by Julie Filippi.[1] The beginning is on familiar lines but with the addition that the princess's pride caused her to be hated by her people. There is the usual muster of suitors but the story differs from the norm in that the successful suitor is a late-comer reaching the palace after the rest have been dismissed. The princess likes him but is too proud

[1] Published in *La Revue des Traditions Populaires*, 1907, pp. 321–3.

to accept him without criticism. So she says she might have had him but for a twisted hair in his beard. Her father suggests that she can pull it out in fun after the wedding but the suitor feigns meekness, goes down on his knees, and begs her to pull out the offending hair then and there. She pulls out a single hair at random and consents to the match. They are married at once but without the full religious ceremony. Meanwhile the father and the husband of the bride have a private talk together and among other things fix the date of the church wedding, which is to take place in the bridegroom's country. Bride and bridegroom leave immediately and travel to the bridegroom's palace. The bride goes to sleep and in her sleep she is conveyed to a shepherd's hut where mean clothing is set out by her bedside. When she wakes she finds she is in a room along with sheep, dogs, and three white-bearded old men. She is terrified and asks where she is, in answer to which the youngest of the three, calling her daughter, expresses wonder that she no longer recognizes her home but dreams she is a king's daughter and a prince's wife. They all laugh when she protests, and her apparent father tells her to get up and go with her grandfather to take the beasts out into the fields, where he and her uncle will join them. She has to obey and before long gets used to the country life and really believes that her old life was a dream. After three months, when the church wedding was due, she is conveyed in her sleep to the palace and wakes up in rich surroundings and attended by four maids. At first she cannot believe in the new setting, and when the three old men come in and bow to her she calls them father, uncle, and grandfather. And so in a way they are, for that is their true relationship to her husband. Then her father appears, the wedding is celebrated, and the princess, now cured of her pride, became in due course a model queen.

I do not suggest that Shakespeare derived his own combination of the two themes used in his Induction and main plot from a version of this Corsican story and I think that the duplication is fortuitous. And yet there is just the chance I may be wrong. That Shakespeare knew some version of the King Thrushbeard story is probable: and in one detail at least the Corsican version is closer to Shakespeare than the others. Only in it does the proud girl want to marry the bridegroom for his own sake. Shakespeare does not tell us explicitly that Katherina wants from the first to marry Petruchio; but when it comes to the point she does not oppose the betrothal, and when the bridegroom is late she gets into a passion of grief. Moreover, in *A Shrew* Kate in a soliloquy confesses she is ready to marry Ferando. There is nothing improbable in Shakespeare's transferring the appearance and reality theme from the princess in the Corsican story to the drunkard in his own Induction. So I think there is just an off-chance of derivation. But even if there were none, it is diverting to see the world's master dramatist and a humble teller of tales in wild Corsica hitting on the same conflation.